SPACE
500
QUESTIONS
AND ANSWERS

Anne Rooney

ARCTURUS

This edition published in 2022 by Arcturus Publishing Limited
26/27 Bickels Yard, 151–153 Bermondsey Street,
London SE1 3HA

Author: Anne Rooney
Illustrators: Jake McDonald and Señor Sanchez
Supplementary Artworks: Shutterstock
Editors: William Potter and Violet Peto
Designer: Sarah Fountain
Design Manager: Jessica Holliland
Managing Editor: Joe Harris

ISBN: 978-1-3988-1463-9
CH008649NT
Supplier 29, Date 0222, Print run 11804

Printed in China

INTRODUCTION

Have you ever looked up into the night sky, at the vastness of space, and pondered its great mysteries with questions like these ...

Why is Mars red?

How big is the universe?

Is there a hidden planet in the solar system?

How long does sunlight take to reach us?

Have we ever heard from aliens?

Where does it rain diamonds?

Who played golf on the Moon?

In this book, you'll find the answers to hundreds of cosmic questions like these, about our Earth, other planets, space missions, comets, asteroids, stars, galaxies, and bizarre black holes.

Are you ready for a journey to the extremes of the known Universe? Yes? Then, turn the page, space ace!

WHAT WAS THE FIRST OBJECT SENT INTO SPACE?

The first object sent from Earth into space was a satellite named Sputnik, launched on October 4, 1957 from the USSR.

What did Sputnik look like?
Sputnik was a shiny metal ball, just 58 cm (23 in) across with four long radio antennae.

Where did Sputnik go?
It was blasted into orbit around the Earth, where it whizzed round at 29,000 km/h (18,000 mph). It made 1,440 orbits, each taking just 96.2 minutes, before burning up as it re-entered Earth's atmosphere on January 4, 1958.

Did Sputnik broadcast anything?
For three weeks, Sputnik transmitted beeps that could be picked up even by amateur radio enthusiasts. It stopped transmitting when its batteries ran out.

WHOSE MUSIC WAS PLAYED ON MARS?

The first music ever broadcast from Mars was a song by the American singer and rapper will.i.am of Black Eyed Peas.

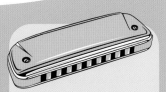

Could anything hear it on Mars?
NASA's Curiosity rover broadcast the song back to Earth, but didn't take speakers—so if there is any life on Mars, it didn't get to hear the music.

What was the first musical performance in space?
US astronauts Walter Schirra and Thomas P. Stafford were the first people to play musical instruments in space. They played "Jingle Bells" on an eight-note harmonica, accompanied by some bells, while orbiting Earth on Gemini 6A in 1965. They pretended to be a UFO called Santa Claus.

HAS ANY SPACECRAFT LEFT THE SOLAR SYSTEM?

Voyager 1 and 2 are the only spacecraft that have left our solar system.

How far have the Voyagers journeyed?
Both Voyagers were launched in 1977. Voyager 1 is now 21 billion km (13 billion miles) away.

How long will the Voyagers continue on their journeys?
The Voyagers will carry on going at 48,280 km/h (30,000 mph) forever, unless they are destroyed in a collision.

How long will the Voyagers continue to operate?
The Voyagers' instruments will send back data to Earth until around 2030, when their power supplies will fail.

How long does it take for sunlight to reach Voyager 1?
Voyager 1 is so far from the Sun that it takes 18 hours for sunlight to reach it. The spacecraft travels at 17 km (11 miles) per second.

Each Voyager carries a golden record holding sounds and photos from Earth and showing where Earth is in the solar system and galaxy.

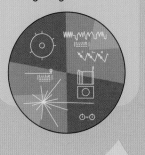

Could the Voyagers leave our galaxy?
The Voyagers could never leave the galaxy, even in billions of years, because they're too slow to escape its gravity.

Voyager 2 is still the only probe to have investigated Uranus and Neptune.

How long does it take to get a message from Voyager?
The Voyagers are still in contact with Earth. A radio message now takes 18 hours to get here.

When will the Voyagers reach another star?
It will be 40,000 years before either Voyager comes even slightly close to another star.

COULD THE APOLLO 11 ASTRONAUTS HAVE GOT STUCK ON THE MOON?

It was possible, yes. The Apollo 11 Moon landing was a difficult and dangerous mission for its astronauts. Success wasn't guaranteed.

What if they could not get off the Moon?

The US president at the time, Richard Nixon, had his speech written in advance, just in case:

"These brave men, Neil Armstrong and Edwin Aldrin, know that there is no hope for their recovery. But they also know that there is hope for mankind in their sacrifice."

But of course the mission was a success.

WHAT HAPPENS TO LIQUIDS IN ZERO G?

There is zero gravity in a spaceship, so liquids don't stay where they are put. They crawl up the sides of a cup or out of the top of a bottle, and float around in the air.

So, how do astronauts take a drink?

Astronauts can suck liquid from a pouch, or use a specially designed cup that uses capillary action—the liquid sticks to the walls of the container and is naturally drawn upward. You can see capillary action at work if you put a sponge in a bowl of water—the liquid moves upward into the sponge.

HOW CAN YOU MAKE A SPANNER IN SPACE?

Since 2014, the International Space Station (ISS) has had a 3D printer so that the crew can make tools or spare parts that they need.

Don't astronauts carry a tool kit?

Yes, but they can't take everything! Space launches are expensive, so taking material that can be turned into tools when needed makes more sense than taking lots of tools that might never be used.

Can tools be recycled?

Yes. A "refabricator" recycles printed items. A tool can be printed, used, then melted down and printed into something else.

WHICH COSMONAUT HAS A COSMONAUT DAD?

The Russian cosmonaut Sergei Volkov.

His father, Aleksandr, was also a cosmonaut. Sergei is the only second-generation cosmonaut or astronaut in the world.

Have there ever been siblings in space?

Yes! Identical twins Scott and Mark Kelly both visited the International Space Station at the same time, in 2011. Scott was part of a Russian mission, and Mark flew with the US shuttle Endeavor.

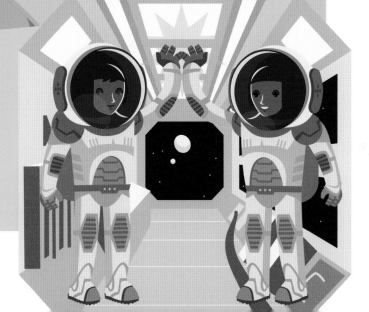

CAN YOU FLY TO MARS IN A STRAIGHT LINE?

No. When spacecraft go to Mars, they have to loop around the Sun in a curved path that meets up with Mars.

Astronauts couldn't just do their thing on Mars and then leave. They'd have to wait months for the planets to be in the right places for the return journey.

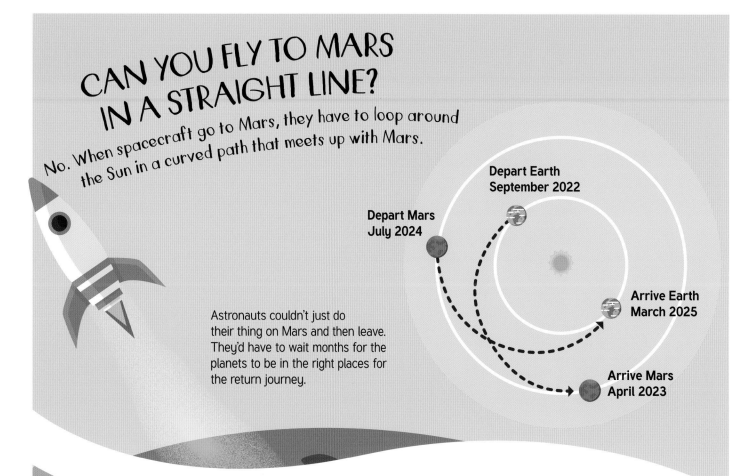

Depart Earth September 2022

Depart Mars July 2024

Arrive Earth March 2025

Arrive Mars April 2023

DOES VENUS HAVE A TROPICAL JUNGLE?

No, but people used to think so. Venus is closer to the Sun than Earth, so it seems reasonable that it would be warmer.

Until the 1960s, people imagined Venus as either a world covered by a warm ocean with maybe a few islands, or a swampy planet inhabited by strange, exotic animals and plants.

Is the surface of Venus wet?
When the USSR sent the Venera probes to explore Venus, they were designed to land in water. In 1967, Venera 4 even had a lock made of sugar that would dissolve on contact with water, to release an extra communications antenna. Now, though, we know Venus' surface is rocky —and there are only traces of water.

WHAT CRAFT WAS FIRST TO FLY PAST JUPITER?

The Pioneer 10 spacecraft, launched in 1972, was the first to fly past Jupiter in 1973. It then headed for the edge of the solar system.

Aquila constellation

Is Pioneer still sending signals?
It hasn't been in touch with Earth since 2003 when its battery power failed, but it will continue onward unless it crashes into something.

Where is Pioneer headed?
The next star in its path is Aldebaran, but it will take 2 million years to get there. Pioneer 10's twin, Pioneer 11, will pass near a star in the constellation Aquila (Eagle) in 4 million years.

WHO WAS THE FIRST HUMAN IN SPACE?

The first human being in space was the Russian Yuri Gagarin on April 12, 1961.

He spent just 108 minutes in space as pilot of the Soviet spacecraft Vostok 1.

Did Gagarin get his mother's permission?
No. Gagarin didn't tell his mother he was going because the mission was top secret.

Did Gagarin tell his wife?
He didn't tell his wife the true date of his flight, but instead told her a later date (by which time he was home). Just in case, he left her a letter saying he didn't expect to return and she should remarry if he died.

HOW DO ROVERS LAND ON MARS?

The latest planetary rovers lower themselves to the surface with a special "sky crane" that they bring along.

It looks like a puppet being lowered by a flying puppeteer.

How does the landing work?
The rover and crane use a parachute to come down through the planet's atmosphere, firing rockets toward the surface to slow them down. Then, the crane gently lowers the lander by a cable to the surface.

What happens to the crane?
The crane has a bad ending. It cuts the cables and flies away, before crashing into the planet's surface.

At only 1.5 m (5 ft) across, it's not easy to spot from 384,000 km (239,000 miles) away.

HAS A SATELLITE EVER GOT LOST?

The first Indian spacecraft to go to the Moon, Chandrayaan-1, went missing in 2009 when it stopped broadcasting signals back to Earth.

Chandrayaan-1

Moon

How was the satellite found?
With interplanetary radar used to track asteroids, NASA finally found Chandrayaan-1 in 2016.

So, where is it now?
Chandrayaan-1 is in orbit 200 km (124 miles) above the surface of the Moon. It could stay in orbit for about 20 years before crashing into the surface of the Moon.

WHAT HAPPENS TO OLD SPACECRAFT?

When spacecraft fail to reach their destination, they don't just disappear —they end up going around the Sun.

How many old spacecraft are in solar orbit?
At least 65 spacecraft and spacecraft parts are currently going around the Sun.

What kinds of spacecraft have ended up in solar orbit?
They include old probes that have done their job (or got lost on the way), satellites that are still working hard and also lots of smaller parts, such as sections and panels dropped by rockets going to the Moon.

How long will they stay in orbit?
The junk could keep going round for millions or billions of years.

IS THERE A CAR IN SPACE?

Yes. In 2018, US businessman Elon Musk launched a red Tesla Roadster into space as a test load for the new Falcon Heavy rocket.

Is it a working car?
Yes. Before blasting it to space, Musk used the electric car to commute in Los Angeles, USA.

Is anyone driving the space car?
It's "driven" by a dummy in a spacesuit. A plaque on the engine reads, "Made on Earth by humans."

Will it break any speed limits?
The car will reach a maximum speed of 121,600 km/h (75,600 mph). Parts of it could last for billions of years, but in a few hundred million years its orbit will change. It might dive into the Sun or be thrown out of the solar system.

ARE ASTRONAUTS THREATENED BY SPACE DUST?

Micrometeors are tiny particles, only a fraction of an inch long. Although they're tiny, they can do serious damage as they slam into spacecraft at huge speeds.

How can astronauts stay safe from the particles?
Spacecraft and satellites need a bulletproof coat to protect them. Often, this is a layer of light metal over a layer of Kevlar (a heatproof material), on top of the spacecraft's outer shell.

What happens when a micrometeor hits the shield?
A micrometeor is usually smashed to dust on the outer metal, and the force of the impact is spread out by the spacecraft's protective coat.

HOW FAR DID NASA'S FIRST MERCURY ROCKET TRAVEL?

NASA's first Mercury rocket flew to only 10 cm (4 in).

What was the rocket's mission?
The Redstone-Mercury rocket, launched in 1960, was the first attempt to launch a spacecraft that could carry a probe to Mercury.

Did the rocket have a crew?
This mission had no crew, but an escape module at the top was designed to blast to safety in a failed launch. On crewed missions, it would carry the astronauts away from the disaster.

Did the rocket fall over?
No. The rocket rose only 10 cm (4 in) before its engines cut out and it settled back on to the launch pad. The escape rocket then fired and rose to a height of 1,200 m (4,000 ft) and landed 370 m (400 yd) away.

Was there a risk of an explosion?
Engineers considered shooting the fuel tanks with a rifle to release pressure and prevent an explosion. They decided against this risky course of action and instead just waited for the battery to run out.

COULD MINING HAPPEN ON ASTEROIDS?

A company based in California and Belgium intends to start mining asteroids for valuable metals and minerals.

What is the company planning?
It's designing a spacecraft that will capture asteroids and drag them through space to a space station (not yet built) for processing.

Why do they need a space station?
They hope the station will become a layover for craft journeying between planets to stock up on fuel, oxygen, water, and other useful supplies.

Just going out for a spin. Don't wait up!

WHO WAS THE FIRST WOMAN IN SPACE?

The Russian cosmonaut Valentina Tereshkova became the first woman in space in 1963, with a three-day trip on Vostok 6.

Did she tell her mother?
Tereshkova's mother found out about her daughter's trip only when she saw the latest pictures from space on television. Although the picture was grainy, it was obvious to her that it was Valentina. She knew her daughter had taken parachute training—but that's all!

WHAT ARE ROVERS?

Rovers are exploration devices that travel over the surface of other planets and the Moon.

Which rover has gone the farthest?
The rover that has gone the farthest is Opportunity, on Mars. It covered 45 km (28 miles) between January 2004 and June 2018, at a stately pace of 180 m (193 yd) per hour.

In second place is the Soviet Lunokohd 2, which journeyed 36.4 km (22.6 miles) across the Moon in 1973.

Which rover is the least adventurous?
The Chinese Yutu rover on the Moon moved only 100 m (106 yd) from its landing site.

WHAT WAS OSIRIS-REx'S MISSION?

The probe OSIRIS-REx was launched in 2016 to explore and retrieve samples from an asteroid.

Was it successful?
Yes! It reached the asteroid Bennu in 2018, and mapped its surface for two years.

How does it collect samples?
It blows puffs of nitrogen gas at the asteroid to dislodge bits of it.

How much material did it collect?
OSIRIS-REx collected 400 g–1 kg (0.8 lb–2.2 lb) of sample material.

How will the samples get back to Earth?
In 2023, after its two-year journey back to Earth, the probe will drop the capsule with the samples and go into orbit around the Sun forever.

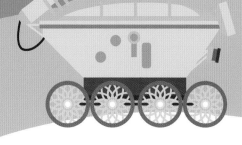

WHY DO ROCKETS HAVE STAGES?

Rockets are designed in stages, with whole chunks used just for carrying the fuel for the first part of the journey.

That means they can be dropped as soon as the rocket has used the fuel.

How many stages were used in the Apollo missions?
The Saturn V rocket, used to launch the Apollo missions, dropped in two stages (which made up most of the rocket). The first part dropped in the first 12 minutes, and the next within three hours.

WHERE IS THE MOST LIKELY PLACE TO FIND LIFE BEYOND EARTH?

The ocean beneath the frozen surface of Saturn's moon Enceladus is one of the most likely places to find life beyond Earth.

What is IceMole?
NASA plans a mission to Enceladus, using a probe called IceMole to melt through some of the ice and take samples. It's already been used to bore through ice in Antarctica.

IceMole can look after itself, choosing a route through the ice and avoiding any obstacles it comes across.

What is IceMole looking for?
It's not looking for large undersea creatures—maybe tiny microbes at best. But who knows?

CAN YOU BUY A MOON LANDER?

Video games designer Richard Garriott bought the Soviet Luna 21 and its Lunokhod 2 rover in 1993 for US$68,500 —but they are both still on the Moon.

When did the rovers reach the Moon?

The craft were sent to the Moon in 1973. Lunokhod 2 journeyed 36.4 km (22.6 miles) over the Moon's surface before being disabled by dust. It is still used for bouncing lasers off to measure the distance to the Moon.

Lunokhod 2

Garriott claims that he owns the area of the Moon occupied by his craft.

WHO WANTS A ONE-WAY TICKET TO MARS?

By far the hardest part of a trip to Mars is taking off for the return journey. Staying there avoids that problem. When the Mars One Foundation asked for volunteers for a one-way trip, more than 200,000 applied to go.

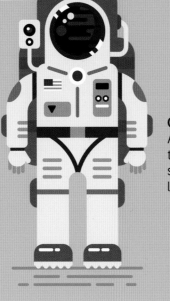

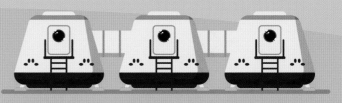

Would you be lonely on Mars?

You wouldn't necessarily be lonely for long. Every 26 months, Earth and Mars are in the right places for another spaceship to fly out, potentially taking more people.

How many people should go?

One space scientist has suggested just one person would go, or maybe a couple.

Could people settle on Mars?

Another organization has plans to set up a colony on Mars, sending groups of people to live there permanently.

IS BEING IN SPACE BAD FOR YOU?

How do your feet cope?
After two months, the hard skin on the bottom of an astronaut's feet has all peeled off, leaving fresh soft skin.

What happens when you cry in space?
If you cry in space, the tears don't fall—they clump together in a big ball that eventually floats away.

Is eyesight affected by time in space?
Eyesight deteriorates, so astronauts who wear glasses often need stronger ones after a few months in space.

What happens to astronauts' muscles?
Astronauts' muscles waste away unless they do lots of exercise—at least two hours a day.

How does space travel affect mental health?
It takes five to ten months to get to Mars, and astronauts will be away for two to three years, cooped up in a small space with other people. It will be emotionally and mentally hard as well as physically demanding.

Are bones affected by lack of gravity?
Bones weaken in space, as they don't have to work as hard without gravity.

Is your heart put under pressure?
The heart shrinks without gravity, as it has less work to do pumping blood around the body.

Identical twins Scott and Mark Kelly have been studied by NASA: Scott spent a year on the ISS while Mark stayed on Earth, and their health was compared.

Do you grow in space?
People grow taller in space without gravity dragging them down. After a year in space, Scott Kelly had grown 5 cm (2 in).

In space, some astronauts lose their sense of taste, or their tastes change so that they start to like things they don't usually like, or dislike things they usually like.

Do astronauts get headaches?
On Earth, gravity drags fluid down the body, but in space there's more at the top of the body. This can cause a puffy face and headaches.

DID A GERMAN RUN THE US SPACE PROGRAM?

Yes. Wernher von Braun was one of many German scientists who surrendered to the USA after WWII.

He was taken to America, where he eventually became the first director of NASA.

What did von Braun design?
Von Braun proposed a space station, planned a trip to Mars, and designed the Saturn V rockets that took the Apollo craft into space.

Were the US rockets based on German missiles?
Von Braun designed the German Army's V2 rocket, and based the design for the Saturn V on it.

DOES TIME GO MORE SLOWLY ON THE ISS?

Astronauts age more slowly than people stuck on Earth—but only very slightly.

How much time difference is there on the space station?
An astronaut on the International Space Station (ISS) gains just 1/100th of a second a year.

But time also goes more slowly at high speeds. The ISS moves fast enough to make up for being in space and still gain an advantage.

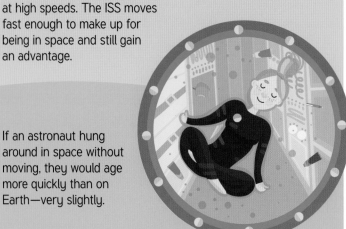

Time goes more slowly closer to a massive object, like a planet, so it should be slower on Earth than on the ISS.

If an astronaut hung around in space without moving, they would age more quickly than on Earth—very slightly.

WHICH ASTRONAUTS JOURNEYED THE FASTEST?

On the way back from orbiting the Moon in 1969, Apollo 10 reached 39,897 km/h (24,791 mph)—the fastest speed ever achieved by a vehicle carrying a crew.

Have uncrewed spacecraft moved faster?
The uncrewed robotic spacecraft Juno reached 266,000 km/h (165,000 mph) as it was pulled toward Jupiter by the planet's gravity in 2014. But the Parker Solar Probe, heading for the Sun, will have a top speed of 692,000 km/h (430,000 mph).

DO OUR SPACECRAFT THREATEN ALIENS?

Every spacecraft carries some microbes from Earth into space, which could be harmful to an alien species.

What harm could the microbes cause?
These could contaminate a planet or moon that might have life of its own, possibly causing harm or changing the course of evolution.

How do we protect aliens?
Under an international agreement, all spacecraft are cleaned super-thoroughly to destroy any microbes. The target is to take no more than 300,000 microbes on any spacecraft.

The Juno spacecraft, sent to explore Jupiter and its moons, plunged into the huge gas giant at the end of its mission so that it couldn't ever crash into one of the moons that might host some form of life.

WHAT ANIMALS HAVE BEEN INTO SPACE?

Two Russian dogs, Veterok and Ugolyok, spent 22 days on Kosmos 110 in 1966, setting a record.

The first monkey to reach space was Albert II in 1949, but he died on the return journey.

A mouse survived going up into space in 1950, but the rocket fell apart coming back and it died.

What was the first dog in space?
The most famous animal in space was a Russian stray dog, Laika, in 1957. She died on the flight.

Lots of different animals have been into space, including spiders, chicken embryos (in their eggs), newts, jellyfish, bees, and even Mexican jumping beans (there's a worm inside the bean).

In 1959, two monkeys called Able and Baker survived a 16-minute flight and returned safely.

Two dogs, 42 mice, two rats, a rabbit, and a collection of fruit flies all went around the Earth on Sputnik 5 in 1960 and came back safely.

What were the first living things sent into space?
The first living things sent into space were tiny fruit flies in 1947. They returned safely.

Have animals been around the Moon?
Zond 5 made the first orbit of the Moon in 1968, carrying two Russian tortoises, mealworms, wine flies, plants, seeds, and bacteria.

Can any creatures survive outside a space station?
Water bears are tough microscopic creatures. They've survived being outside in outer space, where they're freezing cold, bombarded with radiation, and have no oxygen.

HAVE JELLYFISH GONE INTO SPACE?

In the 1990s, astronauts bred more than 60,000 jellyfish on the Space Shuttle Columbia to investigate how they use gravity.

Jellyfish have a special organ to tell them which way up they are.

Tiny crystals roll around in a pocket lined with little hairs. The way that the hairs are disturbed tells the jellyfish which way is up and which way is down.

In the microgravity of space, there is no up or down, so the jellyfish that were bred there never learn to "read" the movement of the hairs.

What happened when they returned to Earth?
When they came back to Earth, their bodies couldn't understand gravity and they remained forever confused.

WHAT WAS THE FIRST CRAFT TO SEND DATA FROM ANOTHER PLANET?

In 1970, the Soviet spacecraft Venera 7.0 arrived at the planet Venus—but it didn't get a soft landing.

What happened to Venera 7?
Its parachute ripped and collapsed on the way through the acidic atmosphere, and Venera slammed into the scorching surface of Venus.

It sent back data on its way down, but then crashed and rolled over so that its antenna was not pointing toward Earth.

How long did Venera 7 survive for?
It seemed to go silent, but a week later, scientists reviewing the tapes discovered it had carried on sending a weak signal for 23 minutes, gaining its place in the record books.

WHICH ANDROID IS BUILT FOR MARS?

NASA'S Valkyrie (or R5) is a human-like robot, 1.9 m (6 ft 2 in) tall and weighing a hefty 136 kg (300 lb).

What roles will Valkyrie have?
It will work alongside astronauts on Mars, building shelters, mining for resources, and helping out with any potential problems.

What else can Valkyrie do?
It can walk, see, use its hands—and put up with terrible working conditions.

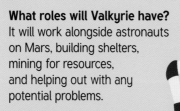

What was the first humanoid space robot?
The first humanoid robot in space was Robonaut 2.0, used on the International Space Station from 2012.

Robonaut originally had no legs, but has been given two "climbing manipulators." Robots in space are good for carrying out tasks that would be too dangerous for humans.

WHO SPENT THE MOST TIME IN SPACE?

Cosmonaut Valeri Polyakov spent nearly 438 days on Mir in a single visit in 1994–1995. That's more than a year and two months.

Who has spent the most time outside a spacecraft?
Russian Anatoly Solovyev has spent the longest time outside a spacecraft in space.

He's made 16 space walks, adding up to more than 82 hours and 10 minutes.

Who spent the most time in space all together?
Cosmonaut Gennady Padalka has spent a total of 878 days in space over five missions on the ISS and the Russian space station Mir.

WHAT STATIONS ARE IN SPACE?

The first space station was Mir, from 1986. Intended to last five years, it survived 15 years, until 2001.

Are space stations sent into orbit in one piece?
Space stations are built in space, from bits launched separately. They are too big to launch ready-built.

Mir was still going after the country that built it had stopped existing—the USSR broke up in 1991, but Mir lasted another ten years.

Can you see the ISS?
The International Space Station can be seen with the naked eye as a bright spot when it passes overhead. (Check **https://spotthestation.nasa.gov** to find out when you can see it.)

Mir went around Earth 86,000 times before breaking up and falling into the sea, and over Canada, Australia, and southern South America.

Is there a US space station?
America's only space station, Skylab, was always called an "orbital workshop." NASA hoped to build a massive space station and didn't want anyone to think that Skylab was it, so they never referred to it as a "space station."

Have astronauts ever gone on strike?
Forced to work 16-hour days, the last Skylab crew staged a small rebellion. They turned off the radio link with Earth and took a day off.

What happened to Skylab?
Skylab was turned off in 1979 and tumbled to Earth. A 17-year-old Australian claimed a $10,000 prize offered by an American newspaper for finding part of it. Chunks of the falling Skylab hit his house.

Although Skylab lasted five years, from 1974 to 1979, it had crew for only 171 days of that time.

DOES EARTH HAVE CRATERS LIKE THE MOON?

Mercury, Mars, and Venus are pitted with huge craters. So is the Moon—but Earth has very few. It's not because the Earth isn't hit by things, but because its surface "heals."

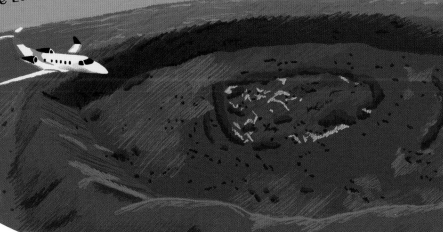

Where do all the craters go?
Wind, rain, moving ice, flowing floods, rivers, and the seas all wear away the surface of the Earth, so craters are soon smoothed out. But some are still visible.

The Vredefort crater in South Africa was 380 km (236 miles) across when it was first created by a massive space rock 2 billion years ago.

It's about a third of the size of Germany.

DO MANY SPACE ROCKS HIT EARTH?

Meteors bombard Earth constantly, but most are too small to see.

What happens to most meteors?
Big, small, and teeny tiny bits of rock collide with Earth every day, but as they whizz through the atmosphere they get so hot that they burn up completely.

If they are big enough, we see these burning meteors as shooting stars.

What's the difference between meteors and meteorites?
The bits of meteors that make it to Earth's surface are called meteorites. They're not all big lumps of rock or metal. Most are micrometeorites, so tiny you need a magnifying glass or microscope to see them.

WHAT'S THE INSIDE OF THE EARTH LIKE?

We live on the Earth's crust— the rocks and water that make up the land and seabed. It's just a thin skin over the top of the planet.

Crust

Lower mantle

Upper mantle

Outer core

Inner core

The crust occupies just 1/100th of the volume of the planet. It's about 30 km (18 miles) thick under land and 5 km (3 miles) thick under the oceans.

Beneath the crust, a thick layer of very hot, molten, semi-liquid rock called magma oozes slowly around the planet.

What's in the middle of our planet?
Right in the middle, Earth has a super-hot iron core. The outer part of it is molten, and the inner part is a solid ball.

The crust is divided into chunks, like pieces of broken eggshell. These are called tectonic plates.

The tectonic plates are carried very slowly around the Earth as they float on top of the magma.

tectonic plates

tectonic plates

How high does our atmosphere go?
The breathable atmosphere is the outermost layer of Earth. It's a very thin wrapper, mostly within 16 km (10 miles) of the surface.

Where the edges of the tectonic plates meet, volcanoes and earthquakes are common.

Plates moving suddenly can cause an earthquake.

What is most of the Earth made of?
Most of the volume of Earth is magma—it makes up about 84 percent of the planet.

IS THE EARTH ROUND?

Earth isn't a true sphere—it's more like a ball that has been squashed from top and bottom, making the middle a bit fatter and the Poles a bit flatter.

What is the name of Earth's shape?
This shape is called an "oblate spheroid," and the podgy bit is called the "equatorial bulge."

Why does Earth have a bulge?
As the Earth spins on its axis, the forces acting on it push more matter toward the equator.

6,357 km
(3,950 miles)

6,738 km
(3,963 miles)

21 km
(13 miles)

If we measure the Earth pole-to-pole and around the equator, the diameter at the equator is 42.7 km (26.5 miles) larger than the diameter at the poles.

IN WHICH DIRECTION DOES THE MOON MOVE?

When we look up at the Moon, it seems to move across the sky from east to west during the night.

If you could stand on the Moon and look back at Earth, it wouldn't move across the sky.

The same side of the Moon always faces the Earth, so you would be looking straight at it all the time—unless you were on the wrong side, in which case you would never see Earth at all.

Why does the Moon appear to move during the night?
Because the Earth is rotating, your place on Earth moves in relation to the Moon as the Earth turns around. This is the same reason why the Sun rises in the east and sets in the west.

DOES THE MOON GO WANDERING?

The midline of the Earth—its fattest point—is called the equator. You might think the Moon would orbit Earth above the equator, but it doesn't stick to that path.

How far does the Moon stray?
The Moon can stray up to 28.5 degrees above or below the equator over a month.

What effect does the Moon's movement have on Earth?
The Moon wandering about affects the tides. Instead of all high and low tides being equal, some high tides are higher than others, and some low tides are lower than others.

When the Moon is directly above a bit of coast, that area will have higher tides than usual.

DOES EARTH HAVE A SECOND MOON?

Earth has a micro-moon called 2016 HO3, which only counts as an asteroid. It shares Earth's orbit around the Sun and seems to loop around Earth all the time, too.

Where is 2016 HO3?
It's about 38 times as far away as the Moon, and is only 40–110 m (120–300 ft) across. It was spotted in 2016.

Moon

Why is it not a moon?
HO3 is called a "quasi-satellite." It's not close enough or permanent enough to count as a real moon.

Earth

HO3

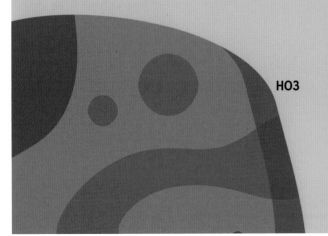

How long has 2016 HO3 been in Earth orbit?
It's been hanging around Earth for about 100 years, and will stay with us for several more centuries before drifting away.

WHY IS IT COLDER AT THE POLES?

The rays that bring light and heat from the Sun strike Earth from straight above near the equator, but from a lower angle in the sky elsewhere.

Sun's rays

Most direct sunlight

Equator

Why does the angle of sunlight matter?

At the poles, the same amount of sunlight is spread out over a greater area of land, so it has less of a heating effect.

Between the poles and the equator, the Sun's rays come from somewhere between straight above and low on the horizon, so the temperature is in between very hot and very cold.

DID WE ALWAYS KNOW THE EARTH WENT ROUND THE SUN?

Sun
Mercury
Venus
Earth
Moon
Mars
Jupiter
Saturn

Until about 1600, most people thought the Sun went around the Earth, though now we know the Earth goes around the Sun.

But, what we see in the sky looks exactly the same either way—we can't tell which way things are moving without using mathematics.

People eventually worked out that the Earth moves around the Sun by making calculations and looking carefully at how the planets seemed to move.

Ptolematic model of the Universe

Sun
Moon
Mars
Earth
Mercury
Venus
Jupiter
Saturn

What would Earth be like if the planets orbited around it?

If the Sun and planets all moved around Earth, the planets would be doing a funny little backward-and-forward dance. But we couldn't absolutely prove what was happening until we could go into space and look!

WHAT DOES THE EARTH GO AROUND?

Earth goes around on its own axis and it goes around the Sun. And then the Sun and the whole solar system go around the Milky Way.

Why do we have leap years?
Earth turns on its axis every 24 hours, making a day. It goes around the Sun every 365.25 days, making a year. (We collect up the quarter days and have an extra day in a leap year, every four years.)

What are you doing?

It's a leap year...

Does the solar system move?
The whole solar system goes around the middle of the Milky Way, but that huge circuit takes 230 million years to complete. Last time we were right where we are now, the dinosaurs were just getting started!

HOW FAST ARE WE MOVING?

If you stood still at the equator, just Earth's rotation on its axis would mean you'd be moving at 1,600 km/h (1,000 mph). You don't notice it because everything else is moving, too.

Our solar system

Milky Way

How fast does the Earth go around the Sun?
The Earth is moving around the Sun at 108,000 km/h (67,000 mph), and the Sun is moving through the galaxy at a speed of 790,000 km/h (490,000 mph). It's enough to make you dizzy!

ARE SATELLITES FALLING OUT OF ORBIT?

Satellites are in orbit above the Earth all the time, but they're also constantly falling.

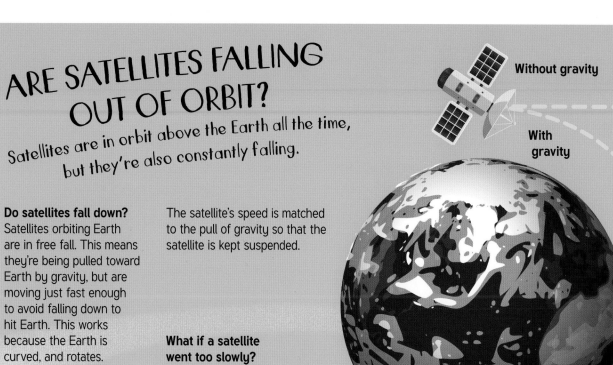

Without gravity

With gravity

Do satellites fall down?
Satellites orbiting Earth are in free fall. This means they're being pulled toward Earth by gravity, but are moving just fast enough to avoid falling down to hit Earth. This works because the Earth is curved, and rotates.

The satellite's speed is matched to the pull of gravity so that the satellite is kept suspended.

What if a satellite went too slowly?
If it went too slowly, it would fall down. If it went too fast, it could whizz off into space.

IS SPACE JUNK A PROBLEM?

Just as there's too much trash on Earth, there's also too much of it in space.

How much junk is in space?
Around half a million bits of "space junk" are tracked as they orbit Earth, moving at speeds of up to 27,350 km/h (17,500 mph). They could do real harm if they crashed into another satellite or a spacecraft, which is why they're tracked.

What is most space junk made of?
Most space junk is bits and pieces of old satellites that no longer work, and discarded parts of rockets that are dropped when no longer needed.

How big are the pieces of junk?
There are 20,000 pieces larger than a tennis ball, 500,000 larger than a marble, and millions of smaller chunks.

DID LIFE BEGIN OFF EARTH?

Some scientists think tiny microbes, carried on comets or asteroids, or just floating around in space arrived on Earth to start life.

Have we found any space microbes?
So far, we haven't found any microbes on asteroids or comets. The theory that life has been spread through the universe by comets and space dust is called "panspermia." It could explain life in many different star systems.

How could space microbes have started life on Earth?
Microbes from outer space could have landed on Earth, and Earth could have had just the right conditions for it to flourish —meaning life on Earth could have evolved from aliens!

WHY DO WE HAVE SEASONS?

Earth is tipped over in its orbit around the Sun. This means that the northern half of the world is tilted 23.5 degrees toward the Sun for part of the year, and the southern half is tilted toward the Sun for the opposite part of the year.

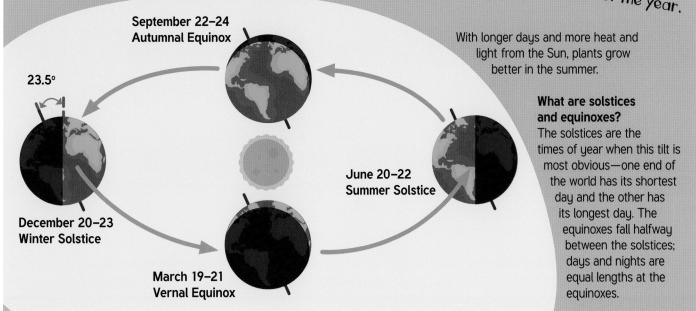

23.5°

September 22–24
Autumnal Equinox

December 20–23
Winter Solstice

March 19–21
Vernal Equinox

June 20–22
Summer Solstice

With longer days and more heat and light from the Sun, plants grow better in the summer.

What are solstices and equinoxes?
The solstices are the times of year when this tilt is most obvious—one end of the world has its shortest day and the other has its longest day. The equinoxes fall halfway between the solstices; days and nights are equal lengths at the equinoxes.

HOW HOT IS THE EARTH?

The middle of the Earth is really hot —about 6,000 °C (10,800 °F). The heat comes from the decay of radioactive material and the leftover heat from the time Earth formed, 4,600 billion years ago.

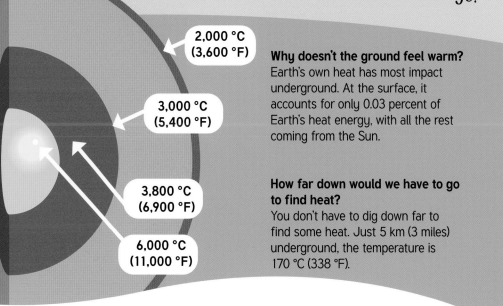

2,000 °C
(3,600 °F)

3,000 °C
(5,400 °F)

3,800 °C
(6,900 °F)

6,000 °C
(11,000 °F)

Why doesn't the ground feel warm?
Earth's own heat has most impact underground. At the surface, it accounts for only 0.03 percent of Earth's heat energy, with all the rest coming from the Sun.

How far down would we have to go to find heat?
You don't have to dig down far to find some heat. Just 5 km (3 miles) underground, the temperature is 170 °C (338 °F).

What would happen if there was no atmosphere?
Without it, a lot of heat would escape at night, and heat would beat down on us during the day (except that we wouldn't be alive without the atmosphere, of course!).

HOW DOES THE EARTH STAY A COMFY TEMPERATURE?

Earth is kept a nice, even temperature by its atmosphere, which traps heat close to the surface.

Without the atmosphere, Earth would be more like the Moon— scorching by day and freezing by night, varying by around 275 °C (500 °F).

What else does the atmosphere do?
The atmosphere doesn't just keep us comfortable. It also saves us from being smashed by meteors. Most burn up in the atmosphere before they reach the ground, but without an atmosphere, Earth would be pitted with craters like the Moon.

WHY IS IT SOMETIMES DARK ALL DAY AT THE POLES?

The Earth is tilted on its axis at an angle of 23.5 degrees. That means the North Pole isn't really at the top and the South Pole isn't really at the bottom.

As a result, each pole is turned toward the Sun for part of the year and away from the Sun for part of the year. In December, the North Pole gets no light at all, and in June, the South Pole gets no light.

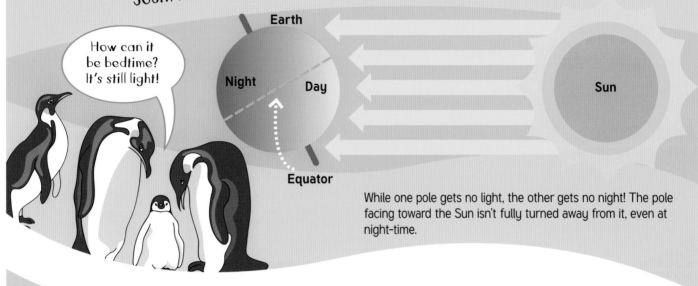

How can it be bedtime? It's still light!

Earth

Night

Day

Equator

Sun

While one pole gets no light, the other gets no night! The pole facing toward the Sun isn't fully turned away from it, even at night-time.

WAS THE EARTH EVER AN ICE PLANET?

Extreme climate change has happened several times in Earth's history, leaving the planet covered in snow.

When did this happen?
About 700–600 million years ago, the whole of Earth's surface was covered with ice, and the average temperature was just −50 °C (−58 °F).

Could life survive at this temperature?
The early life forms skulked deep in the oceans to keep going.

How did Earth heat up again?
Once the surface was all white, it reflected back all the heat from the Sun and so it couldn't warm up again. It could have gone on forever, but Earth's volcanoes came to the rescue. They poured out carbon dioxide that trapped heat and slowly warmed the Earth again.

WHEN WAS THE WORST WEATHER ON EARTH?

As snowball Earth melted, ice turned to water and evaporated, leading to the worst weather ever.

What kind of weather?
Massive hurricanes tore across the land, waves 100 m (300 ft) tall smashed into the coast, and a torrential rainstorm lasted at least 100 years.

Darling, we're not moving to Earth—the weather is dreadful!

How bad was the rain?
Water from the ice mixed with carbon dioxide from the volcanoes to make acid rain. It was so powerful it dissolved the rocks it fell on to, changing the geology of Earth.

DID EARTH LOSE ITS ATMOSPHERE?

Earth had a different atmosphere long ago—but lost it. The first atmosphere was formed of mostly hydrogen-based gases, like the gas giants are now.

How did the atmosphere change?
Lots of volcanoes erupting in the Earth's youth poured different gases into the atmosphere, so that it became mostly nitrogen, carbon dioxide, and water. That was the second atmosphere.

How did we get our current atmosphere?
Finally, tiny oxygen-producing bacteria began to change the atmosphere again. They took in a lot of the carbon dioxide and pushed out oxygen. Green plants still do that. Now, our atmosphere is about one fifth oxygen, which is lucky, as we need the oxygen to live.

WAS EARTH'S AIR EVER DEADLY?

All plants and animals living on Earth today need oxygen to breathe—but long ago, oxygen killed off most of the things that were living then.

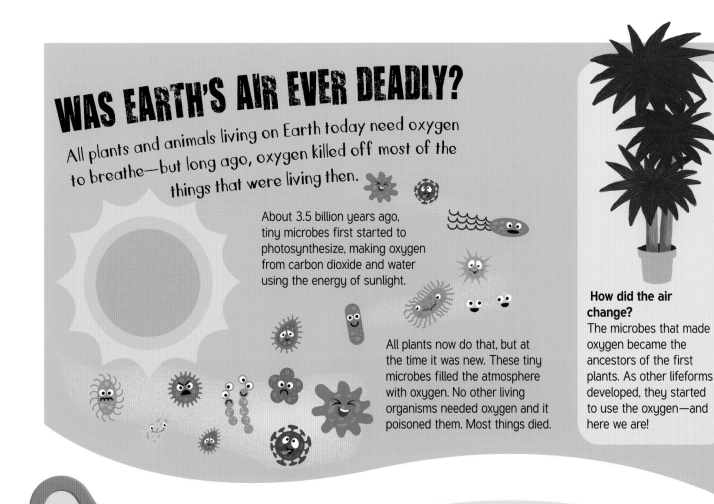

About 3.5 billion years ago, tiny microbes first started to photosynthesize, making oxygen from carbon dioxide and water using the energy of sunlight.

All plants now do that, but at the time it was new. These tiny microbes filled the atmosphere with oxygen. No other living organisms needed oxygen and it poisoned them. Most things died.

How did the air change?
The microbes that made oxygen became the ancestors of the first plants. As other lifeforms developed, they started to use the oxygen—and here we are!

IS EARTH A GIANT MAGNET?

Yes. The Earth's magnetic field is produced by liquid iron moving around solid iron at the Earth's core. This turns the Earth into a magnet, with one magnetic pole near the Geographic North Pole and the other near the Geographic South Pole.

How big is the magnetic field?
The magnetic field extends out into space and affects the solar wind (particles streaming from the Sun).

Does the magnetic field ever change?
Every now and then, the Earth's poles switch around, so the north magnetic pole ends up near the South Pole.

When might this happen next?
The last switch was 780,000 years ago, and many scientists think the Earth is gearing up for another switch. But it takes a long time to happen—more like 1,000 years than overnight!

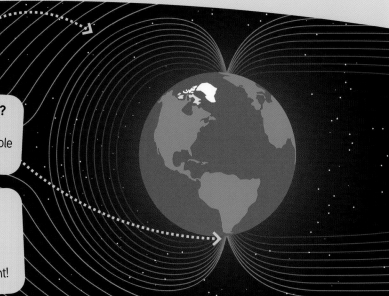

WHAT IS EARTH'S NEAREST PLANET?

Usually it's Venus, but occasionally it's Mars. They swap around.

Mars, Venus, and Earth all orbit around the Sun at different speeds. That means sometimes Mars and Earth are on opposite sides of the Sun, 400 million km (248 million miles) apart.

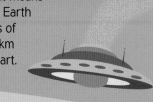

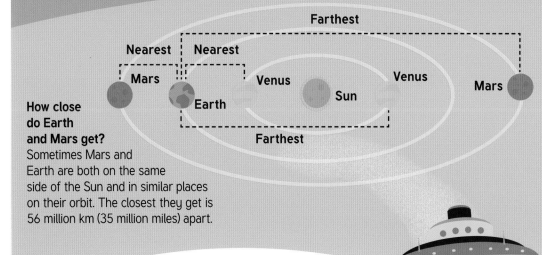

Farthest

Nearest | Nearest

Mars

Earth | Venus

Sun

Venus

Mars

Farthest

How close do Earth and Mars get?

Sometimes Mars and Earth are both on the same side of the Sun and in similar places on their orbit. The closest they get is 56 million km (35 million miles) apart.

How close do Earth and Venus get?

Venus is on a smaller orbit than Mars because it's closer to the Sun. At its farthest, it's 261 million km (162 million miles) from Earth, but at its closest, it's only 40 million km (25 million miles) away.

DOES THE INSIDE OF THE EARTH EVER COME OUT?

Yes. When a volcano erupts, scorching hot, molten rock from inside the Earth pours out through a gap in the surface. While it's inside, it's called magma, but once it's outside, it's called lava.

What else comes out of the Earth?

Along with the lava, superheated water and gases also come out of volcanoes. Volcanoes have helped make the landscape and the atmosphere by bringing material from deep inside the planet up to the surface.

Do other planets have volcanoes?

Yes. Other planets and moons in the solar system also have volcanoes that let some of their insides out. Some spew up hot rock, and some spew out water or ice.

Magma

DOES THE SEABED MOVE?

The oceans have small rifts (cracks) running down the middle of the seabed, through which new rock oozes all the time. Old rock is pushed out of the way by the new rock, so the whole seabed slowly moves toward the shore.

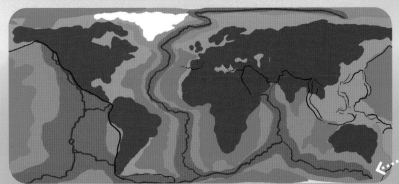

The mid-ocean ridges are shown in red.

Is the seabed flat?
The bottom of the seabed has mountains and valleys, just like the land does.

As the rock of the seabed cools, it slowly sinks lower. At the shore, it sinks beneath the lighter rock of the land and melts, going back into Earth's pool of magma. Very little rock in the seabed is more than 160 million years old.

IS THE ATLANTIC OCEAN GROWING?

The Atlantic Ocean is growing wider at the rate of about 2.5 cm (1 in) a year as new seabed wells up from the middle of the Atlantic Ocean.

How does this affect the continents?
One rift in Earth's surface divides Europe and North America. It runs right through the middle of the island of Iceland, so Iceland is slowly pulling apart.

What about the Pacific Ocean?
On the other side of the world, the Pacific Ocean is getting narrower. One day in the distant future, America and Asia will be pushed together and the Pacific Ocean will close up—but not for hundreds of millions of years.

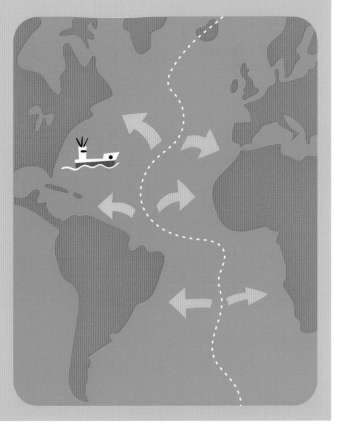

WHERE IS THE EARTH THE COLDEST?

The core of the Earth is scorching, the magma is pretty hot, but the crust is a comfortable temperature to live on. The temperature drops quickly moving up through the atmosphere.

How cold is it in the sky?
The temperature outside a plane in the middle of a flight is around –51 °C (–60 °F). That's just 11,000 m (35,000 ft) above the ground.

What's the average ground temperature?
The average temperature on the ground is 14 °C (57 °F), but there's quite a range.

How cold can it get?
The coldest is –89.2 °C (–129 °F) in Antarctica., and the hottest temperature ever recorded is 70.7 °C (159 °F) in Iran.

HOW ARE MOUNTAINS FORMED?

As the plates of the Earth's crust move around, some crash into each other and the edges are pushed together and upward, making mountains.

Why do we find fish fossils on mountains?
The edges of the plates were previously coastline, so the rock at the tops of the highest mountains was once under the sea. Any fish fossilized in the coastal rock can end up on top of a mountain.

Where are the oldest fossils found?
The rocks inland are much older than the rock beneath the sea, so this is where we find the oldest fossils. The oldest rocks are 4 billion years old—nearly as old as the Earth—although no fossils are quite that old.

IS THERE LIFE ON NEARBY WORLDS?

Dodo

There's been even more life in the past; over 99 percent of all Earth's species that have ever lived have died out.

None of the other planets or moons in the solar system is likely to have life, except just possibly tiny microbes.

Tyrannosaurus rex

Where did life begin?
Life probably started in the water, either deep in the sea or in pools.

How did plants and animals affect the land?
There was no soil on Earth until living things moved on to the land. Soil is made from broken-down plant and animal matter.

How many different species are on Earth?
Earth has lots of life—about 8.7 million different species.

The fact that life started soon after the formation of Earth suggests it gets going easily on a planet with the right conditions.

When did humans appear?
Humans like us appeared only 300,000 years ago.

How long did it take for life to form?
It took just 250–500 million years before chemicals got together and made the earliest life forms …

Everything lived in the water until nearly 500 million years ago.

… but another 3.5 billion years before large life forms started to grow large.

HOW DO YOU MAKE A PLANET IN 4.5 BILLION YEARS?

1 Like all the other planets, Earth started off as dust and gas whirling around the Sun. The dust and gas clumped into lumps.

2 The heaviest material stayed closest to the Sun, making the rocky planets—including Earth.

3 As the Earth-lump spun around and around, it became spherical. The heaviest bits went to the middle, making the iron core.

4 All the rocky planets started in the same way—but they've all turned out a bit different.

5 For 500 million years, Earth was struck by large asteroids and other space lumps.

6 Impact from space rocks and volcanic eruptions kept Earth's surface so hot, the rock was molten and runny.

7 The scalding-hot Earth started to cool and the outside formed a solid crust. Water pooled on the crust, making oceans.

8 Earth's iron core is slowly solidifying. The solid part grows 2.5 cm (1 in) every 25 years—but the molten part is still 2,300 km (1,430 miles) thick.

9 Over the last 100 million years, Earth's layer of molten rock (mantle) has cooled 20 °C (36 °F). It's cooling twice as fast as it used to.

10 Earth will be habitable for another 2–3 billion years. Then, it's likely to drift too close to the Sun and get too hot for life.

Mantle ....

Liquid core ....

Solid core ....

Why was there concern about Jupiter?
In 1994, NASA reported that Jupiter was in danger of being struck by broken chunks of comet.

GREATER GREEN RIVER INTERGALACTIC SPACEPORT

Is there a spaceport on Earth for aliens from Jupiter?

For around 20 years from 1994, the Wyoming town of Green River had the only spaceport set up to welcome refugees from Jupiter.

The residents of Green River worried for the creatures living on Jupiter (if there were any) and decided to welcome them.

What was at the spaceport?
It was the only official intergalactic space port in the world, but it had only a windsock and a welcome sign.

WAS AN OBSERVATORY BUILT TO INVESTIGATE MARTIANS?

American businessman Percival Lowell built the Lowell Observatory in Flagstaff, Arizona, to explore what he thought were "canals" on Mars, when Mars was close to Earth in 1896.

Lowell was enthusiastic about the idea of intelligent life on Mars.

What did Lowell spot instead of Martians?
He photographed Pluto in 1915, but as it was much fainter than he expected, he didn't recognize it.

Who did discover Pluto?
Pluto was officially discovered by Clyde Tombaugh in 1930, at Lowell's observatory.

HOW WAS THE MOON MADE?

Our Moon formed when a small planet or huge asteroid (space rock) crashed into Earth 4.5 billion years ago—only about 100 million years after Earth formed.

One idea is that a small planet smashed into Earth, knocking out a huge chunk that became the Moon. The planet has been called Theia.

Why do scientists think this happened?
The Earth and Moon are made of exactly the same materials, so either the Moon is a chunk of the Earth, or they both formed from the same stuff.

Could it have formed in another way?
Yes, perhaps both Earth and the rogue planet vaporized (turned to gas), and Earth and the Moon both formed from the cooling mixture.

WHAT MAKES OUR MOON SPECIAL?

It's the largest moon belonging to a rocky planet. Mercury and Venus have no moons, and Mars' two moons are tiny in comparison to Earth's Moon.

Are there larger moons in the solar system?
There are only four larger moons in the whole solar system. Three belong to Jupiter and one to Saturn.

Moon	Planet	Mean diameter
Ganymede	Jupiter	5,268 km (3,273 miles)
Titan	Saturn	5,150 km (3,200 miles)
Callisto	Jupiter	4,821 km (3,002 miles)
Io	Jupiter	3,643 km (2,264 miles)
Moon	Earth	3,476 km (2,159 miles)

Only the dwarf planet Pluto has a larger moon for its size, at nearly 12 percent of its mass.

How heavy are moons?
The gas and ice giants have loads of moons, but they never add up to more than one tenth of a percent (0.1 percent) of the mass of their planet. Our Moon, on its own, is 1 percent of the mass of Earth.

WHY IS THE MOON COVERED IN CRATERS?

When was the last big collision?
In 2013, a rock weighing 40 kg (88 lb) hurtled into the Moon at 90,000 km/h (56,000 mph). It made a crater about 20 m (65 ft) across and the flash of the impact was visible from Earth without a telescope.

The Moon has been bombarded by rocks from space (meteors and asteroids) for billions of years, and it's still happening.

Are craters named?
Yes. Example names include Robert, Gaston, and Isabel.

What does the word "crater" mean?
The name was first used by Italian scientist Galileo in 1609. He took it from the Greek word for a cup for mixing water and wine.

Does the Moon have tiny craters?
Yes. The smallest craters are microscopic—too small to see with the naked eye. They have been seen in Moon rocks returned to Earth.

When a space rock crashes into the Moon, rock is blasted out of the surface, some of it melting in the intense heat of the impact.

How old are most of the Moon's craters?
Most craters on the Moon were formed 3-4 billion years ago.

Did we always know about Moon craters?
People once thought the Moon was perfectly smooth; they didn't believe there could be anything imperfect in the heavens.

Craters have a dip in the middle and a wall around the edge.

How long do craters last?
As there is no wind and rain to weather the craters, they remain as they are for billions of years.

What surrounds a crater?
The area outside craters is scattered with smashed rock and beads of glass, made when molten rock cools.

DOES THE MOON HAVE UPS AND DOWNS?

The Moon has highlands and lowlands.
Together, they make the patterns of dark and light
we see when we look at the Moon.

The highlands are the light areas on the Moon's surface, and the low-lying areas are darker, made of rock rich in iron.

Which parts are the oldest?
The highland rock is much older than the darker, lowland rock.

Does the Moon have seas?
Yes, but they don't have water in them. The low areas are flat plains called "maria" (seas). The highlands are called "terrae" (lands). The astronomer Johannes Kepler named them in the 1600s, thinking they were really areas of land and sea.

IS THE MOON PROTECTED?

The sites of the Moon landings are "lunar heritage sites," similar to the "world heritage sites" that are protected special places on Earth.

What can be found there?
The Sea of Tranquility area, with its abandoned Moon junk, will be left as an eternal memorial to our earliest explorations of the Moon.

How is the site protected?
When new probes are sent to crash into the Moon, they are aimed well away from the early landing sites to avoid damaging them.

HOW LONG DO FOOTPRINTS LAST ON THE MOON?

Millions of years! The Moon has very little atmosphere and no weather, such as rain and wind, to wipe out the tracks.

Its surface isn't recycled like the surface of Earth. Nothing changes ...

What marks have humans left on the Moon?
People have left their marks on the Moon in the form of footprints and vehicle tracks in the dust.

What could remove the tracks?
An asteroid or meteor crashing into just the right spot could destroy or cover the footprints—but otherwise they could last millions of years, or even as long as the Moon itself.

IS THE MOON DUSTY?

Yes. It's entirely covered by a layer of small stones and dust called "regolith."

What exactly is regolith?
Regolith is rock that has been ground to dust or small stones by repeated collisions from asteroids and meteors. It's mixed with tiny blobs of glassy minerals formed when molten rocks cooled quickly.

It's because the Moon has a loose, dusty layer that the Apollo missions left footprints and tracks on the Moon. If it was solid rock, there would be none.

How deep is the regolith?
In some of the lowlands, the regolith is just 2 m (6-7 ft) thick, but on the highlands, it can be as deep as 20 m (66 ft).

HAS A SPACECRAFT CRASHED ON THE MOON?

Yes! The Soviet craft Luna 2 was deliberately crashed into the Moon's surface on September 13, 1959. It was the first object from Earth ever to land on another celestial body.

An earlier Luna 1 mission missed the Moon, sailing straight past, and is still moving around the Sun.

How did scientists track Luna 2?
Luna 2 let out a cloud of gas as it neared the Moon that grew to 650 km (400 miles) wide. This let scientists on Earth track its progress by telescope.

How was the explosion planned?
Luna 2 carried two titanium balls made up of five-sided shields called "pennants." An explosive charge in the middle was supposed to blow them apart, scattering the shields over the Moon's surface—but they probably vaporized on impact.

WHEN DID WE FIRST SEE THE FAR SIDE OF THE MOON?

No one saw the far side of the Moon until 1959, when the Soviet spacecraft Luna 3 flew around the back and sent photos of it.

Why do we only see one side of the Moon from Earth?
The Moon takes as long to turn once on its axis as it does to travel all the way around the Earth, so the same side of the Moon is always visible from Earth.

What is the far side like?
The other, hidden, side of the Moon has a much thicker and older crust and many more craters than "our" side. Meteors and asteroids have smashed through the thinner crust on our side, and hot liquid rock has flowed out and renewed the surface. On the other side, the crust is too thick to be punched through by space rocks.

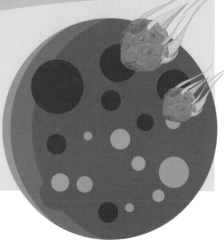

CAN YOU LOSE WEIGHT ON THE MOON?

Yes. Gravity on the Moon is only about one sixth of Earth's gravity. That means that an astronaut who weighs 82 kg (180 lb) on Earth will weigh only 14 kg (30 lb) on the Moon.

What can astronauts do in lower gravity?
Lower gravity means astronauts can leap and bounce in ways they could never do on Earth. But they also fall over more—people need at least 15 percent of Earth's gravity to give their bodies a good idea of which way is "up," so the Moon has barely enough.

Do you get stronger in lower gravity?
No, but everything else weighs less, too, so astronauts can pick up objects that would be far too heavy for them to lift on Earth.

ARE THERE PICTURES ON THE MOON?

People have always seen pictures in the patterns on the full Moon, but they haven't all seen the same thing.

What images have people seen on the Moon?
Some have seen a person with a bundle of sticks, an old man with a lantern, or a woman with a fancy hairstyle and jewels.

Is it always people?
Not always. In China, Japan, and Korea, people see a rabbit making something in a pot—maybe medicine or rice cakes. Other cultures have seen a buffalo, moose, frog, toad, or dragon on the Moon.

DOES THE MOON SHAKE?

Apollo astronauts placed seismometers on the Moon. These are instruments to measure vibrations in the ground. The readings they sent back to Earth showed 28 moonquakes of four different types between 1969 and 1977.

How long do moonquakes last for?
Most earthquakes last just a few seconds, and even the longest are over in two minutes. But, moonquakes can keep on going for ten minutes.

Could quakes affect moonbases?
If we ever build a space station on the Moon, it will have to be made of slightly flexible material so that it isn't cracked by moonquakes.

HOW MANY PEOPLE HAVE LANDED ON THE MOON?

Just 12. Another 12 astronauts have flown to the Moon and around it but have not landed on it. That means only 24 people in total have ever seen the far side of the Moon.

Why did some astronauts not step on to the Moon?
There was always one astronaut who stayed in orbit around the Moon while others landed. The earliest missions didn't have a lander at all.

Did anyone drive on the Moon?
Six of the astronauts also drove rovers, or "moon buggies," over the surface. No one has landed on the Moon more than once.

Who were the astronauts who landed on the Moon?
All 12 people were male, white Americans.

WHAT'S SO AMAZING ABOUT THE MOON?

How far is a lunar orbit?
Flying around the Moon, an astronaut covers the same distance as a plane flying from New York to London.

Does the Moon stay the same distance from Earth?
No, At its closest (called "perigee"), the Moon is 363,300 km (225,740 miles) away. When it's farthest away (called "apogee"), it's 405,500 km (251,970 miles) from Earth.

How fast is the Moon?
The Moon travels around Earth at 1 km per second (0.64 miles per second)—or 3,600 km/h (2,304 mph).

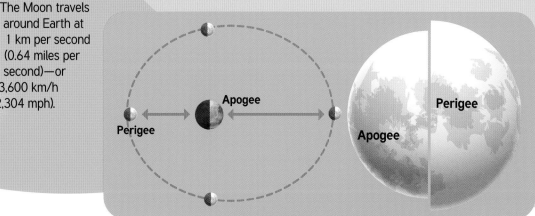

Apogee

Perigee

Perigee

Apogee

Is the Moon as big as a planet?
Our Moon is larger than the dwarf planet Pluto. Pluto is two thirds the size of the Moon at 2,370 km (1,473 miles) across.

Moon

Earth

What is a supermoon?
When the Moon is closer to Earth, it looks bigger. The biggest full moon is 14 percent larger and 30 percent brighter than the smallest. The biggest full moons are called "supermoons."

How big is the Moon compared to Earth?
The volume of the Moon is only 2 percent (1/50th) the volume of Earth.

The first person to calculate the size of the Moon was the Greek mathematician Aristarchus, 2,200 years ago. He thought it was half as wide as the Earth, though it's actually a quarter as wide. Not a bad estimate, though!

Does the Moon have an atmosphere?
The Moon's very thin atmosphere is made of helium, argon, possibly neon, ammonia, methane, and carbon dioxide. It's nothing like Earth's atmosphere, which has just 1 percent argon and tiny amounts of the other gases.

Is the Moon leaving us?
The Moon moves about 3.8 cm (1.2 in) farther away from the Earth every year.

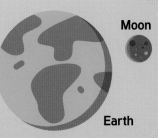

WHO PUT A FLAG ON THE MOON?

The astronauts of the first Moon landing in 1969, Neil Armstrong and Buzz Aldrin, planted an American flag on the surface of the Moon.

How did the flag stay upright?
As there is no wind on the Moon, it wouldn't flutter like it would on Earth and had to be wired so that it didn't just droop down its pole.

Is the flag still there?
The blast from the departing spacecraft blew the flag over. The glorious memorial of humankind's first Moon landing was a bit of a damp squib in the end.

HOW LONG WOULD IT TAKE TO FLY TO THE MOON IN A PLANE?

It's 384,000 km (240,000 miles) from Earth to the Moon, and a Boeing 747 travels at around 965 km/h (600 mph). So, it would take about two and a half weeks to fly to the Moon.

If you could go by car at 80 km/h (50 mph), it would take 200 days—nearly seven months!

Can you fly to the Moon in a straight line?
A rocket going to the Moon doesn't follow a straight path.

Instead, it goes part or all of the way around the Earth and the Moon.

The Apollo spacecraft each took only three to four days to reach the Moon.

WHO PLAYED GOLF ON THE MOON?

The golf balls are still on the Moon.

Apollo 14 astronaut Alan Shepard smuggled a makeshift golf club and two golf balls to the Moon in 1971, hoping to make a record-breaking stroke.

How far did the ball go?
His first shot was disappointing, but the second flew more than 183 m (200 yd), helped by low gravity and no air.

He fixed the head of a golf club to a piece of NASA equipment for collecting rocks. Then he covered the head with a sock so that he could get it on to the spacecraft without anyone noticing.

HOW DOES THE MOON AFFECT TIDES?

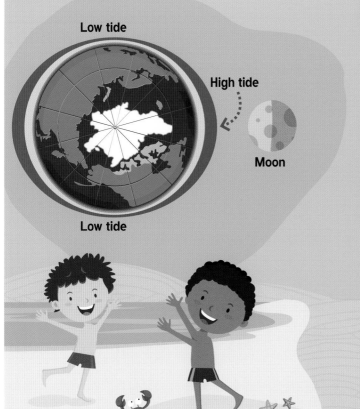

Low tide

High tide

Moon

Low tide

At high tide, the sea comes farther up the beach, and at low tide it doesn't come as far up. This happens because the Moon's gravity is pulling the water!

As the Earth turns, the water on the side closest to the Moon is pulled toward the Moon. The water on the opposite side also "piles up."

How many tides are there in a day?
Each bit of coast has two high tides each day, once when that area is closest to the Moon and once when it's most distant.

IS THERE A DEAD ASTRONOMER ON THE MOON?

Yes, in part. The American astronomer Eugene Shoemaker always wanted to be an astronaut, but a medical problem made it impossible. After he died, his ashes were packed on to the Lunar Prospector lander, which was crashed into the south pole of the Moon on July 31, 1999. He is still the only person "buried" on the Moon.

Did all of Shoemaker make it to the Moon?
Not all of Shoemaker was sent to the Moon—just 28 g (1 oz) of his ashes made the trip, packed into a special capsule wrapped in brass foil, etched with his name and dates.

EUGENE SHOEMAKER

BORN APRIL 28, 1928

DIED JULY 18, 1997

DOES THE MOON HAVE AN ATMOSPHERE?

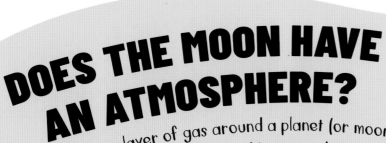

Atmosphere is a layer of gas around a planet (or moon). Our Moon has a very, very thin atmosphere.

How thick is the Moon's atmosphere?
If you collected a jug of Earth-atmosphere and a jug of thin Moon-atmosphere, the Earth-jug would contain 10,000 billion times as many molecules (particles) as the Moon-jug.

I'll leave my helmet on, thanks!

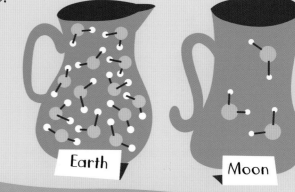

Earth

Moon

Could we breathe on the Moon?
We wouldn't be able to breathe on the Moon, even if the atmosphere was much thicker, as it doesn't have the same gases as Earth's atmosphere.

IS THERE A LOT OF JUNK ON THE MOON?

Astronauts bring very little back, as they need their craft to be as light as possible for take-off. This means that a lot of things get left behind.

Apollo 11 astronauts left a satchel holding medals commemorating two Soviet cosmonauts, who died in 1967 and 1968: Vladimir Komarov and Yuri Gagarin.

For 4.5 billion years, the Moon was a garbage-free zone—then people started going there. Now there's around 180,000 kg (400,000 lb) of clutter there.

A gold pin in the shape of an olive branch (an international symbol of peace) was left as a reminder that the Apollo missions were peaceful.

The hammer and feather from the Galileo demonstration, and Alan Shepard's golf balls (see page 51) are still there.

Tools including hammers, rakes, and shovels were all left behind by the astronauts.

Another commemorative object is a patch from the Apollo 1 mission, which had burst into flames before its launch, killing three astronauts.

A commemorative plaque attached to a leg of the abandoned Apollo 11 lander bears the words:

"HERE MEN FROM THE PLANET EARTH FIRST SET FOOT UPON THE MOON JULY 1969 A.D."
WE CAME IN PEACE FOR ALL MANKIND.

Even expensive cameras were not worth bringing home. A photographer looking for a great vintage camera from the 1970s could find some good stuff on the Moon.

How many vehicles are on the Moon?
We've left more than 70 vehicles on the Moon, including crashed spacecraft, used rovers, and discarded modules of craft.

Is there any gross stuff on the Moon?
Some of the stuff left behind is really not very nice—used wet wipes, empty space-food packages, and 96 bags of human waste and vomit. Yuck!

WHAT ARE OUR CLOSEST PLANETS LIKE?

Mercury

Mars

Earth

Venus

The rocky planets—Mercury, Venus, Earth, and Mars—are nearest the Sun. The gassy planets are far, far bigger and much farther away.

The solar system has four rocky planets and four made mostly of gas or ice.

Uranus

Saturn

Jupiter

Neptune

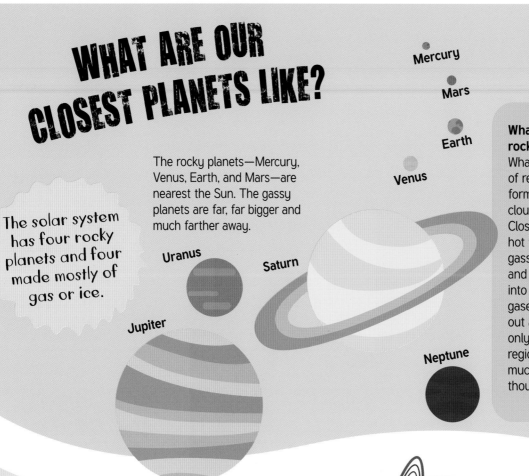

What made the planets rocky or gassy?

What the planets are made of relates to how they formed from the whirling cloud of gas and dust. Close to the Sun, it was too hot for the gases of the gassy planets to condense and then freeze to form into lumps. These light gases were carried farther out and could condense only in a much colder region. Rock can be solid at much higher temperatures, though.

DOES URANUS LIE ON ITS SIDE?

Yes, it's the only planet that does so. It might have been knocked sideways by a collision with something billions of years ago.

How long is a Uranus-year?

Uranus takes 84 Earth-years to orbit the Sun. First one pole and then the other points toward the Sun for 42 years (half a Uranus-year). Just a narrow band near the equator gets a normal day/night sequence for part of the year.

Does it have a north and south?

Its "north" and "south" poles are in the east and west, as its axis (the line about which it rotates) is tilted at nearly 98 degrees.

Uranus has faint rings, which go from top to bottom.

WHAT WOULD IT BE LIKE TO VISIT OTHER PLANETS?

If you could stand on Saturn—which you can't—you would see its rings as bands right across the sky.

Could you survive on Venus?
On Venus, you would be crushed under atmospheric pressure 93 times that on Earth—and you'd be burned by the acidic clouds.

How heavy would you be on Pluto?
On Pluto, you would weigh just 1/15th of your weight on Earth.

Could you stand on Jupiter?
No, as Jupiter has no solid surface. Instead, you would sink 60,000 km (37,000 miles) through gas and then thick, soupy gloop before perhaps reaching a solid core.

How many birthdays would you get on Uranus?
If you lived on Uranus, you would only get one birthday, at the most! As Uranus takes 84 Earth-years to orbit the Sun, only a single whole Uranus-year would pass in a human lifetime.

What are seasons like on Neptune?
If you lived on Neptune, you might spend your entire life in its 80-year summer—but you could be unlucky and spend your whole life in winter.

If you were on Mars, you could watch Earth's transit as it crossed in front of the Sun.

What would you see from a moon of Jupiter?
If you lived on one of Jupiter's moons, such as Europa, Jupiter would loom massively in the sky, far larger than anything we see from Earth.

Does light reach Pluto?
Pluto is 4.8 billion km (3 billion miles) away, so it gets a lot less sunlight than Earth. But it's not completely dark—there's as much light at midday on Pluto as there is on Earth just after sunset.

Is Mercury hot or cold?
Both! You'd need a coat—or a cold drink. The temperature swings wildly between day and night. The side facing the Sun (day) gets scorching hot, at 427 °C (801 °F), and the side facing away (night) gets freezing cold—down to −173 °C (−279 °F).

Where's the best place to see moons?
If you visited Jupiter or Saturn, the sky would be full of moons! Jupiter has 79! They wouldn't all be visible at once, as some would be the other side of the planet—but can you imagine seeing even 30 moons in the sky?

How sunny is it on Mercury?
On Mercury, the Sun would look three times as big as it does on Earth.

Where's the worst place for birthdays?
On the dwarf planet Sedna, you'd only get a birthday once every 11,400 years.

WHO DISCOVERED URANUS?

A German-English amateur astronomer called William Herschel spotted Uranus in 1781.

What did he want to call the planet?
He wanted to name it after the king of England, so Uranus could have been called George.

Did Herschel become rich?
King George was pleased, and gave Herschel a lot of money. Herschel used the money to build bigger and better telescopes, and became a full-time astronomer who made other important discoveries, but he never found another planet.

HOW LONG IS A DAY ON NEPTUNE?

Neptune spins quite quickly on its axis, so its day is just 16 hours and 6 minutes long.

How long is a Neptune-year?
Neptune has more than 87,000 days in its year. It's a long time between birthdays.

When was Neptune discovered?
Neptune was first seen in 1846, which is more than 170 Earth-years ago. But Neptune is so far from the Sun that it takes about 165 Earth-years to go round it once, so it's only just completed one circuit (one year) since it was first discovered. It's the outermost planet of the solar system—so far.

WHERE ARE THE WEIRDEST MOONS?

Which planets have the most moons?

The gas giants have loads of moons: Saturn has at least 61 and Jupiter at least 79. Because the planets are so large, their gravity reaches far into space, letting them capture passing lumps of rock and ice and drag them into orbit as moons.

Which moon is the most volcanic?

Jupiter's moon Io is the most volcanic place in the solar system. It has 400 active volcanoes, some of them shooting smelly fumes of sulfur 500 km (310 miles) out into space.

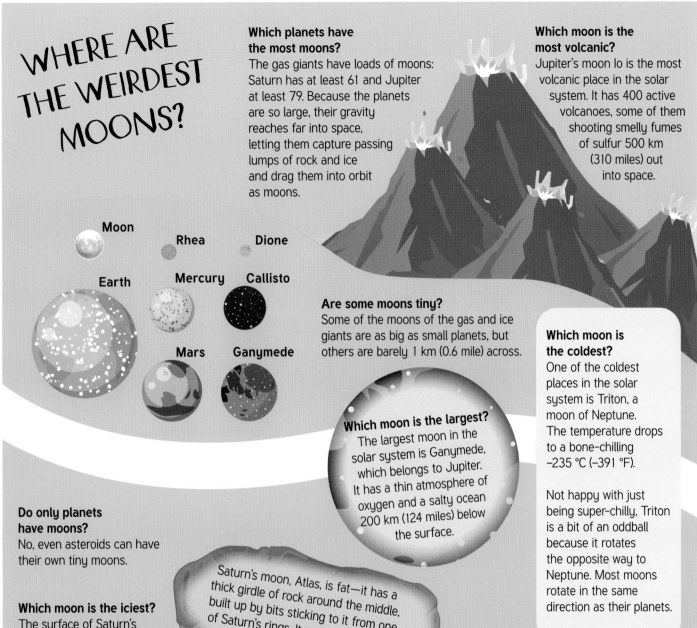

Moon

Rhea

Dione

Earth

Mercury

Callisto

Mars

Ganymede

Are some moons tiny?

Some of the moons of the gas and ice giants are as big as small planets, but others are barely 1 km (0.6 mile) across.

Which moon is the coldest?

One of the coldest places in the solar system is Triton, a moon of Neptune. The temperature drops to a bone-chilling −235 °C (−391 °F).

Not happy with just being super-chilly, Triton is a bit of an oddball because it rotates the opposite way to Neptune. Most moons rotate in the same direction as their planets.

Which moon is the largest?

The largest moon in the solar system is Ganymede, which belongs to Jupiter. It has a thin atmosphere of oxygen and a salty ocean 200 km (124 miles) below the surface.

Do only planets have moons?

No, even asteroids can have their own tiny moons.

Which moon is the iciest?

The surface of Saturn's moon Enceladus is 99 percent water (or, rather, ice). It has ice volcanoes that shoot 250 kg (550 lb) of water into space every second.

Saturn's moon, Atlas, is fat—it has a thick girdle of rock around the middle, built up by bits sticking to it from one of Saturn's rings. It makes Atlas twice as wide as it is tall, at 40 x 20 km (25 x 12.5 miles).

What's inside a moon?

Moons can be rocky or icy. Icy moons often have a liquid layer underneath. Most, maybe all, moons have a solid rocky or iron core right in the middle.

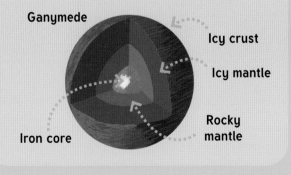

Ganymede

Icy crust

Icy mantle

Rocky mantle

Iron core

HOW THICK ARE SATURN'S RINGS?

Some rings are only 10 m (33 ft) thick, but they are 400,000 km (240,000 miles) across—farther than the distance from Earth to the Moon. There are 500–1,000 separate rings, with some big and small gaps between them.

What are the rings made of?
The rings are made of billions of particles of rock, dust, and ice. These might be solid chunks of rock or perhaps something like dirty snowballs, with smaller lumps frozen together. Some might be the size of a bus, but many are too small to see.

Is Saturn rocky?
Although the rings are rocky, the planet is light and gassy. It could even float in water if you could find a bath big enough.

WHY IS MARS RED?

Mars is known as the red planet. Its surface has red rocks and soil because there's a lot of iron oxide—rust—in them.

Does Mars have moons?
Mars has two moons, but they're tiny. Phobos is 22.2 km (13.8 miles) across and Deimos is just 12.6 km (7.8 miles) across. Both look rather like potatoes —they aren't large enough to have spun themselves into spheres.

Phobos

Deimos

How big is Mars?
Mars is much smaller than Earth—it's 6,791 km (4,220 miles) across, or just over half the width of Earth. Mars would fit inside Earth six times.

WHY IS A VENUS DAY LONGER THAN ITS YEAR?

Venus, the second planet from the Sun, takes 224 days to orbit around it. But it turns on its own axis so slowly that it takes 243 Earth-days to make one full rotation. It doesn't complete even one "day" before it's been right around the Sun.

Which planet has the shortest day?

The shortest day in the solar system is on Jupiter. There, a day is just under ten hours long. And a year is nearly 12 Earth-years long. That means there are more than 10,000 Jupiter-days in a Jupiter-year.

WHERE IS THE LARGEST VOLCANO IN THE SOLAR SYSTEM?

Olympus Mons, on Mars, is the largest volcano in the solar system.

Olympus Mons

How big is Olympus Mons?

It's more than 22 km (13.5 miles) tall, while the tallest mountain on Earth, Mount Everest, is just over a third that size, standing at 8.8 km (5.5 miles) high. Olympus Mons is not only tall—it's 100 times the volume of the largest volcano on Earth.

How much ground does it cover?

As a shield volcano, Olympus Mons has shallow slopes that build up as lava slowly leaks out. That's why it can cover an area the size of France on a planet much smaller than Earth.

Is the volcano active?

Olympus Mons has not erupted for around 25 million years, and appears to be dead.

ARE THE ICE PLANETS COLD?

Uranus and Neptune are called ice giants, but the sludgy ice that gives them their name is not cold —it's scalding hot.

Neptune

Why is the ice hot?
Ice is a name for frozen liquids—normal ice is frozen water. But gases can become ice when they are squashed under such immense pressure that the particles don't have room to move around. The temperature is high, but the particles can't moved so the "ice" doesn't melt.

Can you make "hot ice" on Earth?
Scientists have made "superionic water ice" by squashing water at pressures 2 million times Earth's atmosphere. It doesn't melt until it reaches 4,726 °C (8,539 °F)—much hotter than inside the planets.

Uranus

Methane ice has a blue tinge, which is why Neptune and Uranus look blue.

ARE NEPTUNE AND URANUS SOLID ICE?

They're ice planets, but they're not just big chunks of ice.

What is Uranus made of?
The very top layer is an atmosphere of hydrogen, the same gas as makes up most of Jupiter and Saturn. Below that is a thick layer of water, methane, and ammonia, which probably form sludgy ice. And right in the middle, there is almost certainly a small core of rock and ice.

Atmosphere

Core

Inner mantle

Outer mantle

Methane ice is also flammable, so if there were oxygen, the ice giants could burn.

WHAT ARE COMETS?

Comets are messy lumps of rock and dust glued together with ice.

Where are comets found?
They go around the Sun on a long elliptical orbit.

What makes a comet's tail?
A spectacular glowing tail is made by sunlight falling on gas and dust streaming from the comet's body, as part of it evaporates in the Sun's heat.

Can comets hit planets?
A heart-shaped plain on Pluto was probably caused by a comet smashing into the surface, gouging a hole that has filled with frozen nitrogen. It is 1,600 km (1,000 miles) across.

How big are comets?
The largest known comet, McNaught, is just 25 km (15 miles) wide.

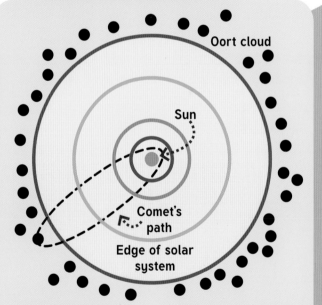

Oort cloud

Sun

Comet's path

Edge of solar system

What is the most famous comet?
Halley's comet is seen every 76 years. Its tail can be 100 million km (60 million miles) long, but the middle is just 8 km (5 miles) across and 16 km (10 miles) long.

Will Halley's Comet last forever?
Each pass by the Sun melts some of the comet, so eventually it will be all gone. Halley's comet loses a layer 10 m (33 ft) thick on each visit, so it will last another 76,000 years.

How many comets are in the solar system?
Trillions of comets live in the Kuiper Belt, beyond Neptune, and come by the Sun (and us) on orbits shorter than 200 years.

Another trillion live farther away, in the Oort cloud at the edge of the solar system. Their orbits take thousands or millions of years.

WHAT ARE COMETS MADE OF?

If you see a comet in the sky, it looks spectacular—a bright, shining speck trailing a long, glowing tail. But close up, they are messy lumps of rock and dust, often shaped like a potato.

The tails always face away from the Sun.

Comets orbit the Sun on a long elliptical orbit. As they get close, some of the ice evaporates and the freed gas and dust make up the tail.

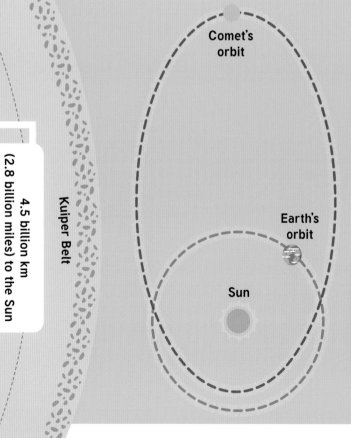

Comet's orbit

Earth's orbit

Sun

Kuiper Belt

4.5 billion km (2.8 billion miles) to the Sun

HOW OFTEN DO COMETS DROP BY?

Many comets come near Earth regularly. They orbit the Sun in a giant ellipse (squashed circle), and we see them when they come close to Earth in their orbit.

What are short-period comets?
Comets that come back within 200 years are called short-period comets. They spend most of their time in an area called the Kuiper Belt, beyond the orbit of Neptune.

What is the Kuiper Belt?
It's a broad band of space 30–55 times as far from the Sun as Earth is, packed with icy lumps. There are trillions of them hanging out there, big and small.

WHERE IS THE WILDEST WEATHER IN THE SOLAR SYSTEM?

The stormiest storm in the solar system occurs on Neptune. Its Great Dark Spot, which was first seen in 1989, had winds of 2,400 km/h (1,500 mph).

How stormy is Jupiter?
Storms on Jupiter can last for hundreds of years. Its Great Red Spot is a storm twice as wide as the Earth.

The Great Red Spot was first seen in the 1600s. The spot we can see now has been visible since 1830. It might be the same one as was spotted in the 1600s, or a new one.

Outside the Spot, winds regularly tear around the planet at nearly 600 m per second (2,000 ft per second).

Which planet is the hottest?
Venus is the hottest planet in the solar system, with a surface temperature of up to 462 °C (864 °F).

How does it get so hot?
Its atmosphere, made mostly of carbon dioxide, traps heat close to the planet in a runaway greenhouse effect.

Even the clouds are bad on Venus —they're made of burning acid that could eat through metal.

Where does it rain diamonds?
Storms on Neptune and Uranus might produce diamond "hail" from carbon under huge pressure.

The diamond rain could have produced lakes or even oceans of liquid diamond, maybe with floating diamond icebergs.

IS THERE ANOTHER PLANET?

Some astronomers think there might be.

Where might it be?
Planet Nine, NASA suggests, could be 20 times farther from the Sun than Neptune. As Neptune is 4.5 billion km (2.8 billion miles) from the Sun, that makes Planet Nine 90 billion km (56 billion miles) away.

What is this possible planet called?
The extra planet is sometimes referred to as Planet Nine. It is too far away to see with a normal telescope.

How big could it be?
Planet Nine is likely to be ten times the mass of Earth. That's big, but much less massive than the gas giants.

How will we find it?
Astronomers are looking for Planet Nine with a huge telescope in Hawaii. It's the best tool we have for finding something small and dark. But they don't even know where to look for it—it could be anywhere in a giant circle around the Sun.

It could take Planet Nine 10,000–20,000 Earth-years to orbit the Sun just once.

Why do we think it exists?
The gravity of Planet Nine—if it's there— would explain the odd activity of some objects in the Kuiper Belt. Some have a very tilted orbit, move at an angle to the rest of the solar system, or orbit the Sun in the wrong direction.

Is Planet Nine affecting the solar system?
Planet Nine could be tilting the entire solar system! The planets and other objects don't orbit in line with the Sun's equator, but at an angle of about 6 degrees.

What might Planet Nine look like?
Planet Nine is likely to be an icy gas planet, like Neptune and Uranus. It would be so far away that it would get very little light or heat from the Sun.

Is Earth in danger from this extra planet?
The myth that an extra planet (often called Nibiru) will soon come from the outer edges of the solar system and destroy Earth is an internet hoax, and it's completely false.

Other stars that have planets often have "super Earths"—planets much larger than Earth but smaller than the gas giants. The Sun notably doesn't have one (unless Planet Nine turns out to be a super Earth!).

WHERE IS OUR NEAREST STAR?

Our Sun is the nearest star, one like millions of others—it just looks huge and bright because it's so close.

What kind of star is the Sun?

The Sun is a common type of star—it's a medium-size, yellow dwarf, main sequence star. That means it's at a healthy stage in the middle of its working life, pumping out energy as heat and light.

What use is the Sun?

The Sun provides all the energy that life on Earth needs. Its gravity keeps Earth and the other planets of the solar system in orbit. We couldn't live without it!

HOW LONG DOES IT TAKE LIGHT TO REACH US FROM THE SUN?

Light moves very, very quickly—it covers nearly 300,000 km (186,000 miles) every second. But the Sun is so far away that it still takes 8 minutes and 20 seconds for its light to get to us.

499 light seconds

If the Sun suddenly exploded or went out (don't worry, it won't!), we wouldn't know about it for just over eight minutes.

How do astronomers measure huge distances in space?

Astronomers measure distances in space in light years.

What is a light year?

The time light can travel in an entire year is called a light year. It's nearly 9.5 trillion km (6 trillion miles). That's 9,500,000,000,000 km (6,000,000,000,000 miles).

WHAT'S SO GREAT ABOUT THE SUN?

How heavy is the Sun?
The Sun weighs 330,000 times as much as Earth.

How old is the Sun?
The Sun is 4.6 billion years old.

How fast does the Sun spin?
The Sun turns once on its axis every 27 days.

How big is the Sun compared to Earth?
Earth would fit inside the Sun 1.3 million times over.

How far away is the Sun from Earth?
The Sun is 150 million km (93 million miles) from Earth. That distance is called an astronomical unit (AU).

It would take six months to fly all the way around the Sun in a jumbo jet.

What's inside the Sun?
Right in the middle, where all the action is, the temperature is 15 million °C (27 million °F).

Where is most of the Sun's mass?
Ninety-eight percent of the Sun's mass is crammed into the middle third of its volume.

The Sun contains 99.8 percent of the mass of the solar system. All the planets, moons, comets, and asteroids make up the rest.

How hot is the Sun?
The temperature at the Sun's surface is 6,000 °C (11,000 °F).

What is the Sun's corona?
The atmosphere around the edge of the Sun is called the corona. It's much hotter than the surface, at 1–10 million °C (1.7–17 million °F). No one knows why.

IS OUR SUN A TINY STAR?

All stars are classed as dwarfs, giants, or supergiants. There's no "normal" stage between dwarf and giant. Stars are dwarf when they are young and healthy, working the way a star should work.

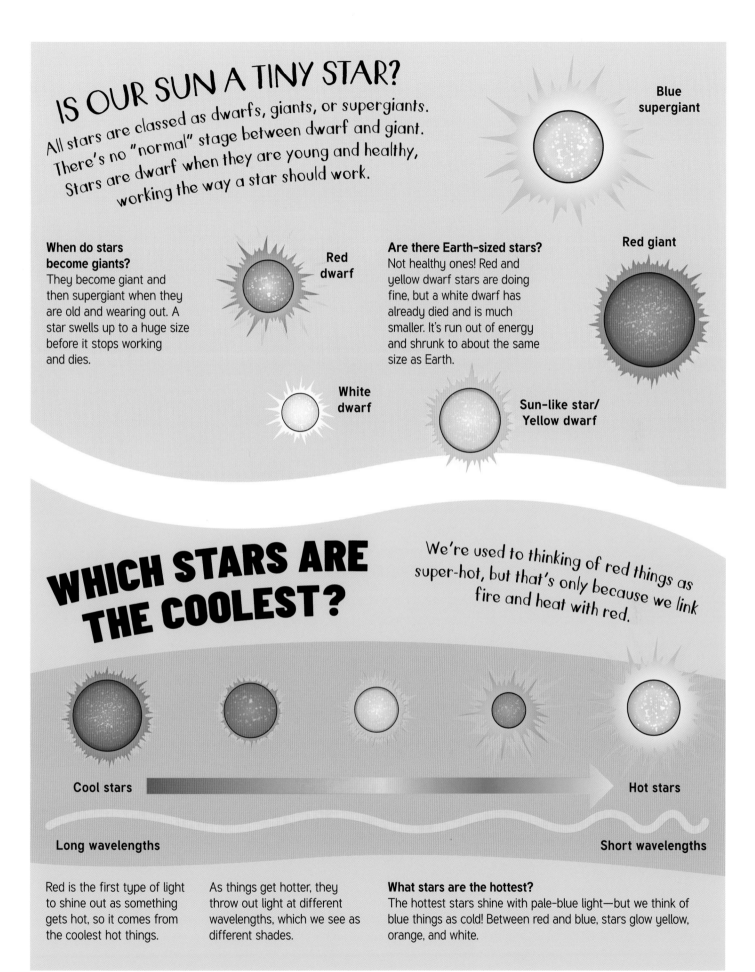

Blue supergiant

When do stars become giants?

They become giant and then supergiant when they are old and wearing out. A star swells up to a huge size before it stops working and dies.

Red dwarf

Are there Earth-sized stars?

Not healthy ones! Red and yellow dwarf stars are doing fine, but a white dwarf has already died and is much smaller. It's run out of energy and shrunk to about the same size as Earth.

Red giant

White dwarf

Sun-like star/ Yellow dwarf

WHICH STARS ARE THE COOLEST?

We're used to thinking of red things as super-hot, but that's only because we link fire and heat with red.

Cool stars ➡ Hot stars

Long wavelengths — Short wavelengths

Red is the first type of light to shine out as something gets hot, so it comes from the coolest hot things.

As things get hotter, they throw out light at different wavelengths, which we see as different shades.

What stars are the hottest?

The hottest stars shine with pale-blue light—but we think of blue things as cold! Between red and blue, stars glow yellow, orange, and white.

HOW DO STARS WORK?

Stars like the Sun give off light and heat energy by messing about with matter in a way that's called "nuclear fusion."

What are stars made of?
All stars are mostly hydrogen gas, one of the two chemical elements that were created at the Big Bang.

What happens in the middle of a star?
At the middle of a star, hydrogen is squashed together under such huge pressure it becomes another gas, called helium.

It takes four atoms of hydrogen to make one atom of helium, but not absolutely everything is used up. The last tiny bit escapes as energy.

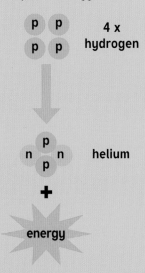

p p
p p   **4 x hydrogen**

↓

n p n   **helium**
   p

+

energy

Although each reaction is tiny, there's enough helium-making going on to release all the light and heat of a star.

p = proton

n = neutron

How long do stars last?
Stars keep going until they have used up a lot of their hydrogen. It usually takes billions of years.

Before they die, they start making different chemicals by fusing the helium.

What happens when a star explodes?
When large stars explode, iron fuses in the explosion, making all the other elements in the universe.

Where do these elements go?
All the elements made in the star in its life and death are scattered when a star explodes.

WHAT ARE SUNSPOTS?

Sunspots are dark patches on the surface of the Sun. They're not really dark—they just look dark compared to the super-bright areas around them.

Are sunspots cold?
Sunspots are cooler than the rest of the Sun's surface. But they're still pretty hot at 4,200 °C (7,700 °F) instead of 6,000 °C (11,000 °F).

How big are sunspots?
They're not small spots— they can be 160,000 km (100,000 miles) across. That's 12 times as wide as the Earth.

ARE THERE PICTURES IN THE STARS?

Pictures made by joining stars together are called constellations or asterisms. Some were first named 3,000 years ago in Mesopotamia (ancient Iraq).

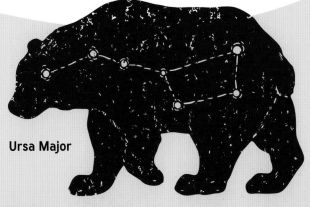

Ursa Major

Do people see the same pictures?
People see different things in the stars. Ursa Major was seen as a bear in Ancient Greece and a wagon in Mesopotamia.

In Burma, it's a prawn or crab, and an Arab story describes it as a coffin followed by three mourners.

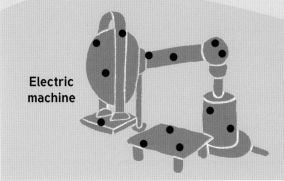

Electric machine

Is there a slug in the night sky?
When Europeans started sailing south and saw unfamiliar stars, they invented new pictures, including "electric machine," "earthworm," "pangolin," and, yes, "slug."

Pangolin

HOW WILL THE SUN DIE?

The Sun won't go with a bang—it's too small for that. In about 5 billion years, when it runs out of hydrogen it can use, the Sun will swell to a red giant, taking in Mercury and Venus.

The surface will be uncomfortably close to Earth.

Will the Sun keep swelling?
No. It will lose its outer layers, leaving a hard, dense white dwarf about the size of the Earth—but still with much of its mass.

Will the Sun cool down?
Gravity at the surface will be 100,000 times Earth's gravity, and it will be 20 times as hot as the Sun's outer parts are now. Heat escapes slowly into space, so it will take trillions of years to turn into a cold, dead black dwarf.

HOW LONG DOES IT TAKE FOR LIGHT TO LEAVE THE SUN?

Light is produced as photons (packets of energy) deep in the Sun. But the Sun is very dense and it takes a very long time for a photon to get out.

Each photon is taken in and kicked out again by one particle after another. It's not heading in any particular direction; it bumbles around randomly.

Inside, the Sun is opaque—the opposite of transparent. It's about as opaque as a rock, so it takes a long time for light to move through it.

A single photon can spend up to 170,000 years wandering from the middle to the surface.

WHAT'S INSIDE A SUPERNOVA?

Inside a supernova, a star collapses to a ball 10 km (6 miles) across. Only a tiny, dense middle is left and the rest is scattered.

The gravity in the core of a collapsed star is so great that all the space is crushed out of it and it becomes solid matter.

Why do supernovas explode?
The largest stars fuse elements up to iron and can then go no further. The core collapses and the energy is so intense it blows the star apart.

Can supernovas become black holes?
If the core is 1.4–5 times the mass of the Sun, it becomes a neutron star. If it has more mass than that, it becomes a black hole.

HOW HEAVY IS A TEASPOONFUL OF NEUTRON STAR?

A teaspoonful of neutron star would weigh tens of millions of tons.

Why is a neutron star so heavy?
All the space has been squeezed out of a neutron star, leaving only the heavy bits of matter crushed together. There's not even space within the atoms.

How fast do neutron stars spin?
Neutron stars spin around super-fast—hundreds of times each second.

How big are neutron stars?
A neutron star with three times the mass of the Sun might be just the size of a small city, but it still has almost the same mass it had as a giant star.

ARE ALL THE STARS WE SEE IN THE MILKY WAY?

Yes. The Milky Way is so vast and the stars in it so bright, that we can't make out stars outside it.

The Milky Way is only one of at least 100 billion galaxies in the universe, all packed with their own stars.

Orion

Is everything we see in the night sky a star?
No. The "star" below Orion's belt and one of the "stars" of Andromeda are both nebulae. They are not single stars but entire galaxies outside the Milky Way. When you look at these, the fuzzy cloud of light you see is collected from hundreds of billions of stars.

Andromeda

Which galaxy is closest to the Milky Way?
Andromeda is the closest galaxy, 2.5 million light years away.

DOES THE SUN HAVE A SPIKY OVERCOAT?

The Sun has a layer above the surface called the chromosphere, which has spiky structures called spicules.

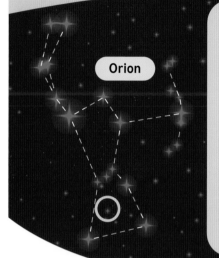

How large are these 'spikes'?
The spikes are 500–1,000 km (300–600 miles) across and grow up to about 10,000 km (6,000 miles) long before they collapse.

How fast are spicules?
Spicules are jets of plasma that burst from the surface at 96 km (60 miles) per second—more than 320,000 km/h (200,000 mph). Each lasts just five to ten minutes. There are about 10 million spicules at any time.

HOW QUICKLY DID OUR SUN GROW?

It took 10 million years for our Sun to grow from a cloud of dust and gas. But then it will live for 10,000 million years—1,000 times as long as it took to grow.

I am the biggest star around here!

Yes, but I'll get to be much older.

Do all stars grow at the same rate?
Some stars grow much more quickly. A few even take just 75,000 years.

Which stars last the longest?
It's not small stars that grow quickly, but really big ones. So small stars grow slowly and have a long and leisurely life, while big stars grow fast, live life in the fast lane, and die young.

IS THE MILKY WAY ON A COLLISION COURSE?

Yes. The Milky Way and the galaxy closest to it, the Andromeda Galaxy, are heading for a crash.

When will they collide?
Andromeda is moving toward us at 110 km (68 miles) per second; the collision is due in about 4 billion years.

Will it be a violent collision?
There's lots of space between stars, so it will probably be a largely peaceful merger with very few stars actually colliding.

Will any other galaxies hit us?
Yes, it could be a three-way crash, as the Triangulum, the third largest galaxy in our Local Group, is moving in the same direction. The new, combined galaxy has already been named: Milkdromeda, or Milkomeda.

ARE BROWN DWARFS STARS?

They're between super-sized planets and tiny stars, but are just too small to work as stars.

Can you see brown dwarfs in the night sky?
Brown dwarfs are very hard to see, as they don't produce much light. They show up with infrared telescopes, though.

How heavy are brown dwarfs?
They have between twice the mass of Jupiter, and just under a tenth the mass of the Sun.

How common are brown dwarfs?
There might be as many brown dwarfs as there are proper, working stars.

Why are they not stars?
Their mass is not enough to kick-start the nuclear fusion that powers stars. But neither are they quite a planet, as they're too big for that.

Do brown dwarfs produce any heat?
Although at the start of their lives, brown dwarfs might have just enough mass to do a tiny bit of fusion, they stop after a few million years and the only heat they produce comes from shrinking because of their gravity.

ARE SOME STARS COOL?

Y-dwarfs are the coldest type of star—or nearly star. They are the coolest brown dwarfs.

How hot are brown dwarfs?
The surface of the hottest brown dwarf could be 750 °C (1,380 °F), but the coolest are just 25 °C (80 °F). That's the temperature of a nice day on Earth.

It's summer on Earth—I want to go home.

We could stop by that brown dwarf if you want a day in the Sun?

There are three classes of brown dwarf.

HOW BIG IS THE MILKY WAY?

The Milky Way is a disk 100,000 light years across—but only 1,000 light years thick.

What type of galaxy is the Milky Way?
The Milky Way is a spiral galaxy. That means it's got a whirling-round shape, with arms trailing out into space.

Where is our solar system in the Milky Way?
There are four main arms and some smaller arms. We are on a smaller arm, 28,000 light years from the middle.

How big is the Milky Way compared to our solar system?
If the solar system out to Neptune's orbit was 2.5 cm (1 in) across, the Milky Way would be as wide as the USA.

How long does it take to move around the Milky Way?
The Sun goes around the middle of the Milky Way at 828,000 km/h (514,000 mph)—one circuit takes 230-240 million years.

HOW MANY STARS ARE IN THE MILKY WAY?

There are up to 400 billion stars in the Milky Way.

No one knew the Milky Way was a massive band of stars until 1610, when it was first seen through a telescope.

What is the future of the Milky Way?
Between 1 billion and 1 trillion years from now, the Milky Way and all the other galaxies of the Local Group will have merged into a single mega-galaxy.

Is the Milky Way part of a larger group?
The Milky Way is part of a group of galaxies called, unimaginatively, the Local Group.

There is probably a supermassive black hole at the middle of the Milky Way.

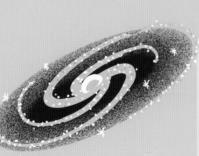

Is the Milky Way just one galaxy?
Two dwarf galaxies are merging with the Milky Way right now, but they don't affect us.

DID THE UNIVERSE BEGIN WITH A BANG?

The start of the universe is called the Big Bang.

How loud was the Big Bang?
The Big Bang was silent—there was no "bang."

How fast did the universe expand?
Everything expanded from a tiny point to the size of a grapefruit in just 0.0000000000000000000000000000001 seconds.

In this time, the universe doubled in size 90 times.

Was it a visible explosion?
There was no explosion to see, either—even if there had been anything with eyes to see it.

What appeared first?
The first bits of matter—nuclei, the middles of atoms—appeared in the first minutes. This was almost all hydrogen and helium.

All space, time, matter, and energy in the universe were created in an instant.

Atoms formed as nuclei combined with electrons.

Where did stars and planets come from?
By this point, clouds of matter clumped into lumps that became galaxies and stars.

Can we see the early universe?
Light first emerged from the darkness after 380,000 years—astronomers can still trace some of it.

Galaxies have different shapes, but lots are spirals with "arms" made by their whirling motion in space.

What came before the Big Bang?
No one knows what, if anything, existed before the Big Bang, or what, if anything, is outside the universe. "Before" and "outside" might be meaningless.

The hydrogen and helium created in the first minutes still power the stars.

One second

Three minutes

380,000 years

1 billion years

13.8 billion years

CAN WE SEE INTO THE PAST?

Yes. Light takes a very, very long time to reach us from distant objects in the sky. If a star is 50,000 light years away, the light we see when we look at the night sky left the star 50,000 years ago.

How long does light take to reach us from the North star?
The North star, Polaris, is 323 light years away, so we see it as it was 323 years ago. If it had exploded in 1900, we wouldn't see the explosion until around 200 years from now.

If any aliens 67 million light years away looked at Earth with a super-powerful telescope, they would see dinosaurs roaming the planet —they would see 67 million years into the past!

HOW OLD IS THE UNIVERSE?

The universe is about 13.8 billion years old, so it will be 14 billion in just 200 million years.

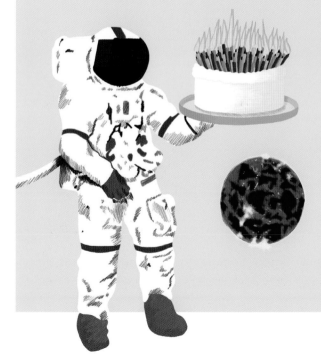

When did the first stars appear?
The first stars probably appeared around 180 million years after the Big Bang. They were the first lights in a previously pitch-black universe.

Are the first stars still shining?
None of those stars still exists, but the light from them is still crossing the universe, so we can see them in the past.

IS THE UNIVERSE GETTING BIGGER?

Yes. The Big Bang was the sudden appearance of everywhere (all space-time). Since then, "everywhere" has been getting bigger.

What did the universe expand into?
It didn't expand into empty space, but space appeared in between the stuff of the universe, pushing it all apart.

If you drew stars on a balloon and blew up the balloon, you would see the same effect—the stars would get farther apart.

Big Bang

5-6 billion years

Is the universe speeding up?
Around 5-6 billion years after the Big Bang, the speed at which the universe was growing bigger increased. So it got bigger more quickly, and is still getting bigger, faster and faster.

How do we know?
If the universe had kept expanding at the same rate (following the red line), it wouldn't be as big as it is now.

CAN THE HUBBLE SPACE TELESCOPE SEE PLUTO?

Hubble can show fantastic detail in a galaxy 72 million light years away, but Pluto look likes a blurry blob in Hubble photos.

Pluto

Distant galaxy

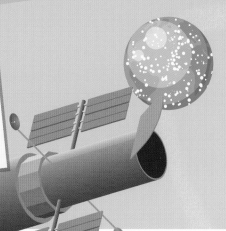

Why does Hubble only see Pluto as a blob?
How much Hubble can see depends on the size of the object, how much light it produces, and how far away it is. A galaxy 50,000 light years across is 4 billion times the size of Pluto. It's packed with stars pumping out light, but Pluto just reflects the light of the Sun from its tiny area.

How far away is Pluto?
At its closest, Pluto is about 5 light-hours from Earth.

HAVE WE EVER SEEN A LIVE SUPERNOVA?

In 2008, a NASA astronomer just happened to be looking at the right bit of space to see a star explode in a supernova at that very moment.

When did the supernova take place?
It was not quite "at that very moment," because it actually happened 88 million years ago.

How fast was the explosion?
The star-stuff exploded outward at 10,000 km (6,200 miles) per second—that's nearly 36 million km/h (23 million mph).

How useful was spotting the supernova?
Catching the first five minutes of a supernova means astronomers now know what to look for. They hope to spot hundreds every year.

WHERE ARE WE IN THE UNIVERSE?

We are right in the middle of the observable universe. That's because "the observable universe" means the parts of the universe we can see, and we can see the same distance in all directions. Therefore, the observable universe has to be a sphere with Earth in the middle.

How big is the observable universe?
We can measure the observable universe—it's 93 billion light years across. But we have no idea how much more universe there is outside that. We could live in a tiny part of a much larger universe, or we might be able to see almost all of it.

ARE BLACK HOLES ACTUALLY HOLES?

Holes are gaps where there's nothing. A hole in your pocket is where there's no pocket and things can fall through. But a black hole is somewhere that has more stuff, not less.

It won't stop pulling me!

So, what is in a black hole?
It's an area where matter is so squashed there is no space in it at all, not even within the atoms.

Gravity is produced by objects with mass, and as a black hole has a lot of mass, it also has a lot of gravity.

What happens if you get close to a black hole?
Anything that gets too close to a black hole is pulled toward it and squashed along with everything else. That's how black holes grow.

IS THERE A BLACK HOLE AT THE MIDDLE OF THE MILKY WAY?

The galaxy has a supermassive black hole in the middle. It has the mass of 4 million Suns and is called Sagittarius A* (pronounced "A-star").

How many black holes are there in the whole galaxy?
There are probably two big ones, the second one having the mass of only 100,000 Suns. These are just the big ones—there are more than 100 million smaller black holes in the Milky Way.

Steer well clear of the middle, Captain!

Do all galaxies have black holes in the middle?
All galaxies probably have a huge black hole in the middle, with the mass of millions or billions of stars crushed into a small space. As they take in more dust, gas, and other matter all the time, they grow ever larger.

Black holes come in three sizes—tiny, small, and huge.

How small are tiny black holes?
Tiny black holes are the size of an atom or smaller.

How do small black holes form?
Small black holes are created after huge stars collapse in a supernova explosion.

Are there no medium-sized black holes?
There don't seem to be medium-sized black holes. They could be at the heart of dwarf galaxies—but dwarf galaxies are hard to see as they're faint and distant. Or there might really not be any medium-sized black holes.

How big are supermassive black holes?
Supermassive black holes exist in the middle of galaxies. They can be billions of times larger than the small black holes.

HOW WILL THE UNIVERSE END?

The universe is still expanding, getting more and more spread out. Where will it end? No one knows for sure.

The end of the universe is not something to worry about; whatever happens could be anywhere from 2.8 billion years away to never.

What if the universe keeps expanding?
The universe could carry on getting bigger quickly until it's just a thin, dark soup of matter where nothing can hold itself together—a Big Rip.

What if the universe shrinks?
The universe could reach a final size where matter is so far apart that there is no movement or heat. Or everything could bounce back toward the middle in a reverse of the Big Bang—a Big Crunch.

WHAT ARE EXOPLANETS?

Exoplanets are planets around other stars.

When were exoplanets discovered?
The earliest evidence of exoplanets is a photo taken in 1917, but its significance wasn't noticed for 90 years.

How do we find exoplanets?
Telescopes in space such as Kepler and the planned James Webb telescope look for exoplanets that might have the right conditions for life.

Where is the nearest exoplanet?
Proxima Centauri, our nearest star, has an exoplanet only 4.2 light years from us.

How many exoplanets do we know about?
Around 4,000 exoplanets have been found so far.

Exoplanet 55 Cancri is half solid and half molten.

What are most exoplanets like?
Most exoplanets are gas planets, like Jupiter and Saturn.

Exoplanets include rocky planets, ice or ocean planets, cold gassy planets, hot gassy planets, and "lava worlds."

How big is the biggest exoplanet we know of?
The most massive exoplanet ever found is called HR 2562 b. It's 30 times the mass of Jupiter, which might be too big for a planet—it could be a brown dwarf instead.

How many planets are in our galaxy?
There are probably more than a trillion planets outside our galaxy.

How long are exoplanet-years?
Exoplanets' "years" range from a few hours to thousands of Earth-years.

Ooh, it's my birthday again!

What was the object?
A splinter of rock 230 m (800 ft) long and 35 m (100 ft) wide. It was named Oumuamua from the Hawaiian for "scout."

HAS OUR SOLAR SYSTEM BEEN VISITED BY AN OBJECT FROM OUTSIDE?

Late in 2017, an asteroid from another star system in the Milky Way whizzed into our solar system, looped round the Sun, and left again.

When was it spotted?
No one noticed it until it had already zipped past Mars, Earth, Mercury, and Venus, gone around the back of the Sun, and was heading away again.

The International Astronomical Union invented a new classification for asteroids from far away: Oumuamua is 1I (I for "interstellar").

HOW DO WE SPOT PLANETS AROUND OTHER STARS?

We look for a star going dim. As a planet passes in front of a star, it blocks a little bit of the light from the star—just as if you hold your hand up in front of a light bulb.

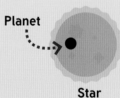

Planet

Star

How do you know it's a planet?
If a star dims at regular intervals, it's taken as a sign of an orbiting planet passing between Earth and the star once every exoplanet-year.

Do planets block a lot of light?
Planets make a tiny difference in brightness, but astronomers can spot that difference using telescopes and computers.

Can we find all the exoplanets in this way?
Only planets on a direct line between Earth and their star will show up. If a planet's too high or low to block light from Earth, we won't know it's there. Only one in 100 exoplanets can be found, the rest stay hidden from sight.

COULD EARTH BE DESTROYED BY AN ASTEROID?

The chance of this happening in the next few hundreds of years is nearly zero.

Could we stop an asteroid hitting Earth if we spotted it?

If we saw an asteroid coming, we might be able to knock it off course or blow it up. But if it was dark, and came sneakily fast with the Sun behind it, or if it came from outside the solar system, it could be here with no warning.

Has there ever been a close call?

A medium-sized asteroid slipped between Earth and the Moon in January 2017. Astronomers didn't spot it until two days before. If it had hit, it would have made an explosion 35 times as large as an atomic bomb.

HOW COLD IS IT IN SPACE?

The temperature in deep space is about -270.5 °C (-455 °F).

How cold is that?

That's only a few degrees warmer than the coldest temperature that is possible anywhere, -273.15 °C (-459.7 °F). At that point, all the particles in matter stop moving—nothing can be colder.

Is it cold throughout space?

Not all of space is freezing. Gas between stars, or the solar wind (stream of particles) from stars, can be very hot, reaching thousands or even millions of degrees.

It's warmer the closer you get to a star. A thermometer in space above Earth, half in the Sun and half in shade, would show about 7 °C (45 °F).

Quick! It's much warmer by that star!

ARE BLACK HOLES SPACE GATEWAYS?

Most astronomers think matter that gets pulled into a black hole is compressed and destroyed. But a few think black holes are tunnels to another universe.

Black hole

White hole

What could be on the other side?
At the end of the tunnel—or wormhole—the matter is spat out of a white hole where it's used to make—well, whatever that universe has in it.

Could they go to another universe?
Our own universe might be at the end of a white hole from another universe. And maybe that one is at the white-hole end of an even bigger universe.

We could be anywhere in a chain of universes linked by wormholes through black holes.

WHERE ARE THE GALAXIES HEADING?

The Earth moves round the Sun, the Sun moves around the galaxy, and the Milky Way, along with the other galaxies in its supercluster, moves toward something called the Great Attractor.

What is the Great Attractor?
No one really knows what it is, but it's 500 million light years across and has a mass 1,000 trillion (1,000,000,000,000,000) times the mass of the Sun.

How fast are the galaxies moving?
Galaxies are hurtling toward it at a speed of 1,000 km (6,200 miles) per second.

Are we going to crash soon?
It's 150 million light years away, so even at that speed, we're not about to crash anytime soon.

IS THE UNIVERSE LIKE A GIANT SPONGE?

The structure of the universe is a bit like the structure of a natural sponge, with large empty spaces surrounded by walls or "filaments."

Where do we live in the sponge?
We live in a hole—the Milky Way is in possibly the largest void in the universe, at 1.8 billion light years across. Obviously, it isn't completely empty—the whole of the Milky Way and other nearby galaxies are in it.

What are the filaments?
The filaments are made of strings of closely related galaxies. The empty spaces have much less in than the densely packed filaments.

HOW BIG IS THE UNIVERSE?

The universe is at least 93 billion light years across. That's how far we can measure—but it could be a lot bigger.

Are we at the edge of the universe yet?

How far can we see?
The edge of the visible universe is 46.5 billion light years away. That should mean the light left it 46.5 billion years ago, but that's not possible as the universe is only 13.8 billion years old.

Because space is expanding, more space is being added all the time between us and the most distant objects. So the light had already come some way toward us when the object was pushed farther back.

Can we measure the universe?
The things that are 46.5 billion light years away might be a long way from the real edge of the universe. We have no way of measuring the whole universe.

IS SPACE MOSTLY EMPTY?

Andromeda is the galaxy nearest to ours, but it's not very near at all—it's 2,500,000 light years away.

As the Milky Way is 100,000 light years across, and Andromeda is 140,000 light years across, there's room for lots of empty space in between.

How big is the Andromeda Galaxy as seen from Earth?
We can't see Andromeda very well because it's not very bright. But if it showed up more clearly, even at this huge distance from us, it would be four times the size of the full Moon in the night sky.

ARE BLACK HOLES HARD TO SPOT?

We spot black holes by seeing matter go around them or spotting the signs of matter going toward them. But if a black hole has cleared out its local area already, there's nothing to see.

Does that mean there are lots of hidden black holes?
Scientists think there might be up to ten times as many black holes as we know about, just because they're sitting there doing nothing.

I'm not lazy! I've finished all my work!

What will happen to these so-called "lazy black holes"?
They will eventually go away, very slowly leaking radiation until they evaporate to nothing. But it takes a long time.

How long would they take to disappear?
A black hole the mass of the Sun would take 10^{67} years (that's 1 followed by 67 zeroes) to disappear.

WHEN DID WE DISCOVER OTHER WORLDS?

People first saw the planets as disks in 1609. Until the telescope was invented, no one could see that the planets are worlds rather than spots of light.

Was the idea of other worlds dangerous?

The idea that ours might not be the only world was revolutionary. Italian philosopher Giordano Bruno was burned at the stake in 1600 for (among other radical new ideas) suggesting there could be other worlds with other beings.

How could they tell the difference between stars and planets before 1609?

Before the telescope, the way the planets move, and don't twinkle, showed they're not the same as the stars. But that's all anyone knew.

Even in 1609, telescopes weren't powerful enough to show what the five visible planets were like—that three are rocky and two are made of gas.

IS THERE MORE THAN ONE UNIVERSE?

Some scientists suspect we're part of a multiverse—an infinite number of universes that branch off all the time.

What does an infinite number of universes mean?

This means all possibilities become real. There's a universe in which you had toast for breakfast and one in which you didn't.

There's a universe in which Earth is dominated by three-eyed blue creatures, and many universes in which Earth doesn't even exist.

Our universe might be just one in a bubbling pot of many, many universes.

COULD WE TRAP ALL THE SUN'S ENERGY?

A Dyson sphere is an imaginary mechanism for trapping all the energy from the Sun to use on Earth.

Never mind that we don't actually need anywhere near that much energy, science likes a challenge.

How would a Dyson sphere work?
The sphere would wrap the Sun with solar panels to catch the energy it produces.

Do Dyson spheres exist?
It might sound silly, but it's possible that alien civilizations are building them. When astronomers found stars that lose their brightness by up to 65 percent every so often, one suggestion was something like a Dyson sphere harvesting energy from them.

Just as well we remembered to leave a gap to get in and out!

HOW DO YOU RATE ALIEN CIVILIZATIONS?

The Kardashev scale gives six levels of technological progress for alien worlds, 0–5.

A type-0 civilization only harnesses some of its home planet's energy.

A type-1 civilization could use all available energy on its home planet.

A type-2 civilization could control its star and use all of its energy.

A type-3 civilization could use energy from and travel across a galaxy.

A type-4 civilization could control the energy of the entire universe.

A type-5 civilization would be like gods, able to do anything at all.

Where does Earth sit on the scale?
We don't even rate 1 on the scale—we have a level-0 civilization because we don't all cooperate (have a global society) and we don't use all the solar energy that falls on our planet.

WHAT IS A PULSAR?

A pulsar is a rapidly rotating neutron star, left behind after the death of a star 20 times the mass of the Sun.

Was the first pulsar named after aliens?

Yes. A research student called Jocelyn Bell found the first pulsar in 1967. She discovered regular radio pulses that repeated every 1.34 seconds. It seemed too regular to be natural, so was named "LGM" for Little Green Men in case it was an alien radio signal.

How does a pulsar act?

It works a bit like a lighthouse, sending out a beam of radiation every time it goes around.

How fast do pulsars spin?

Some pulsars spin faster than the blades in a food processor—hundreds of times a second.

IS A LIGHT YEAR THE BIGGEST MEASUREMENT THERE IS?

No. When we want to measure the size of galaxies, even light years aren't big enough. Galaxies are millions or billions of light years across.

What's longer than a light year?

The biggest unit astronomers can use is the gigaparsec—which is a billion parsecs. A parsec is 3.262 light years, or about 31 trillion km (19 trillion miles). Earth is 14 gigaparsecs from the edge of the observable universe.

What about measuring huge volumes in space?

Cubic parsecs can be used to measure volume. The number of stars or galaxies in a cubic parsec shows the density of matter in space.

The Sun is the only star in its cubic parsec. But in globular clusters of stars there can be 100–1,000 stars in a cubic parsec.

It's just a few parsecs to Grandma's house!

CAN A STAR SWALLOW ANOTHER ONE WHOLE?

A rare kind of star called a Thorne–Zytkow object is a red supergiant with a working neutron star inside it.

How do these occur?
Both might be formed in a supernova, but the neutron star is absorbed by the much larger supergiant.

Can neutron stars merge?
Yes. Sometimes, two neutron stars merge with each other. When they do, they make heavy metals.

How much metal do they make?
Two neutron stars with the combined weight of three Suns merged in 2017, producing 3 to 13 times the mass of the Earth in solid gold!

HAVE WE ALREADY HEARD FROM ALIENS?

The "Wow! signal" arrived in 1977.

Why is it called the "Wow! signal"?
It's called the "Wow! signal" because the astronomer who spotted it wrote "Wow!" on the printout.

Everything about the signal is odd, leading astronomers to wonder if it was sent by aliens.

What was odd about the signal?
It was unusually loud, standing out against background radio noise. It was over a short bandwidth, just as our own deliberate radio broadcasts are. It was at just the right frequency for interstellar transmissions—one that would attract attention.

Has it been heard since?
It went on for 72 seconds and was never found again. It's still unexplained, more than 40 years later.

WHAT WAS THE FIRST SPACE TELESCOPE?

Where is Hubble?
Hubble orbits 547 km (340 miles) above Earth, going around the world every 97 minutes.

How fast does it travel?
It travels at 8 km (5 miles) per second. It could travel across the USA in ten minutes.

Hubble was the first telescope sited in space to look at distant objects. It launched on the Space Shuttle Discovery in 1990.

When was the idea of a space telescope suggested?
The first suggestion for a space telescope was made in 1923, before the first rocket had been launched.

What happens if Hubble breaks down?
Hubble is serviced and repaired in space by astronauts on spacewalks.

How many pictures has Hubble taken?
Hubble has produced hundreds of thousands of images of space objects. It sends 120 gigabytes of data back to Earth every week.

Any astronomer in the world can apply for a slot of Hubble's time to look at whatever they want.

Seen by Hubble, the stars don't twinkle.

Hubble focused on a small area of nearly empty space for 114 days—and found nearly 10,000 galaxies.

The most distant galaxy spotted by Hubble is 13.8 billion light years away.

HOW MANY STARS ARE IN THE UNIVERSE?

There are many more stars in the universe than grains of sand on Earth. Our galaxy probably has around 400 billion stars.

How is this number worked out?
There are probably between 100 billion and a trillion galaxies. If they were all a similar size, there would be at least 400 billion x 100 billion stars, which is 20 sextillion (20,000,000,000,000,000,000,000) stars.

Has someone counted all of Earth's sand grains?
Of course not, but researchers in Hawaii worked out the area and depth of all the world's beaches and the volume of a grain of sand. Then they calculated that there are 7.5 quintillion (7,500,000,000,000,000,000) grains of sand on Earth.

So there are more than 2,500 times as many stars as there are grains of sand.

WHEN DID HUBBLE HAVE A PROBLEM?

Immediately! As soon as the Hubble telescope was in space, a fault in the mirror showed up.

How was it repaired?
It took the most ambitious spacewalk ever to repair it. After 11 months of training to prepare for it, seven astronauts flew into space.

What was wrong with the mirror?
It was uneven—but only by 1/50th of the thickness of a sheet of paper. Even that was enough to make the images blurry and poor—no better than could have been gained from Earth.

HUBBLE TELESCOPE

Instruction Manual

With five days of space walks and repairs, Hubble was fixed and—three years after launch—finally produced stunning images.

WHERE IS THE WORLD'S LARGEST RADIO TELESCOPE?

The largest radio telescope with a single dish is in China; it's 500 m (1,650 ft) across.

How is it affected by visitors?
Tourists using cell phones near radio telescopes disrupt the work it does and can make the telescopes useless.

How can this disruption be stopped?
There's a 5-km (3-mile) zone around the telescope where people aren't allowed to use their phones, but it's a hard rule to enforce.

Are there even larger telescopes on Earth?
Bigger radio telescopes are made by linking antennae in widely spaced dishes. They're called array telescopes. The biggest is ALMA in Atacama, Chile. It has 66 dishes that can be spread over 16 km (10 miles).

IS SOME OF THE UNIVERSE MISSING?

Adding up all the bits we know about, we can account for only 1/20th of the total mass of the universe.

How much of the universe is a mystery?
Only 1/20th of the universe is made of the normal matter we see in our bodies, other objects, and planets like Earth. Ninety-five percent is unknown.

Dark matter: 27%

Normal matter: 5%

What could the rest of the universe be made of?
The rest is made of dark energy (68 percent) and dark matter (27 percent). No one really knows what they are.

What could dark matter be?
Dark matter could be lots of brown dwarfs or patches of dense matter that don't emit light. Or it could be a type of matter we have never met.

Dark energy: 68%